BIOLOGY AND CRIME

Volume 10
SAGE RESEARCH PROGRESS SERIES IN CRIMINOLOGY

ABOUT THE SERIES

The SAGE RESEARCH PROGRESS SERIES IN CRIMINOLOGY is intended for those professionals and students in the fields of criminology, criminal justice, and law who are interested in the nature of current research in their fields. Each volume in the series—four to six new titles will be published in each calendar year—focuses on a theme of current and enduring concern; and each volume contains a selection of previously unpublished essays . . . drawing on presenta-tions made at the previous year's Annual Meeting of the American Society of Criminology.

Now in its third year, the series continues with five new volumes, composed of papers presented at the 30th Annual Meeting of the American Society of Criminology, held in Dallas, Texas, November 8-12, 1978. The volumes in the third year of publication include:

- *Biology and Crime*
  edited by C. R. Jeffery
- *Perspectives on Victimology*
  edited by William H. Parsonage
- *Police Work: Strategies and Outcomes in Law Enforcement*
  edited by David M. Petersen
- *Structure, Law, and Power: Essays in the Sociology of Law*
  edited by Paul J. Brantingham and Jack M. Kress
- *Courts and Diversion: Policy and Operations Studies*
  edited by Patricia L. Brantingham and Thomas G. Blomberg

Previously published volumes include *Violent Crime: Historical and Contempo-rary Issues* (James A. Inciardi and Anne E. Pottieger, eds.), *Law and Sanctions: Theoretical Perspectives* (Marvin D. Krohn and Ronald L. Akers, eds.), *The Evo-lution of Criminal Justice: A Guide for Practical Criminologists* (John P. Conrad, ed.), *Quantitative Studies in Criminology* (Charles Wellford, ed.), *Discretion and Control* (Margaret Evans, ed.), *Theory in Criminology: Contemporary Views* (Robert F. Meier, ed.), *Juvenile Delinquency: Little Brother Grows Up* (Theodore N. Ferdinand, ed.), *Contemporary Corrections: Social Control and Conflict* (C. Ronald Huff, ed.), and *Criminal Justice Planning and Development* (Alvin W. Cohn, ed.).

Comments and suggestions from our readers about this series are welcome.

SERIES EDITORS:

James A. Inciardi
University of Delaware

C. Ray Jeffery
Florida State University

SAGE RESEARCH PROGRESS SERIES IN CRIMINOLOGY
VOLUME 10

biology and crime

Edited by C. R. JEFFERY

Published in cooperation with the
AMERICAN SOCIETY of CRIMINOLOGY

 SAGE Publications   Beverly Hills   London

For information address:

SAGE PUBLICATIONS, INC.
275 South Beverly Drive
Beverly Hills, California 90212

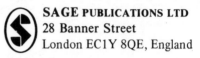

SAGE PUBLICATIONS LTD
28 Banner Street
London EC1Y 8QE, England

Printed in the United States of America

Library of Congress Cataloging in Publication Data

Main entry under title:

Biology and crime.

(Sage research progress series in criminology; v. 10)
"Published in cooperation with the American Society of
Criminology."
Bibliography: p.
  1. Criminal anthropology—Addresses, essays, lectures. 2.
Criminal psychology—Addresses, essays, lectures. 3. Socio-
biology—Addresses, essays, lectures. 4. Deviant behavior—
Addresses, essays, lectures. I. Jeffery, Clarence Ray, 1921-
II. American Society of Criminology.
HV6115.B54   346.2'4   79-14490
ISBN 0-8039-1277-3
ISBN 0-8039-1278-1 pbk.

FIRST PRINTING

CONTENTS

C. R. Jeffery
Florida State University

1

BIOLOGY AND CRIME
The New Neo-Lombrosians

The theme of the 1978 annual meeting of the American Society of Criminology (held in Dallas, Texas November 8-12) was Criminology: International and Interdisciplinary. As I have argued elsewhere, criminology is an interdisciplinary field, but due to historic misfortune sociology captured the field in the 1920s. The contributions of biology and psychology have been minimized, while at the same time major developments have occurred in these fields. Biology has entered what has been characterized as the "era of the new biology," following the work of Watson and Crick in 1953 on the biochemical basis for inheritance. Joining biology and chemistry led to the greatest scientific revolution since quantum physics was put forth by Einstein, Planck, and Bohr. We are now in the midst of a major revolution concerning genetics as seen in cloning and genetic engineering. Our knowledge of biology is so far ahead of our knowledge of law and society that major conflicts are now occurring over such issues as abortion, the right to die, and human subject experimentation.

Kevin Phillips, a political commentator and analyst, said on an NBC news program that the 1978 elections involved issues related to the politics of biology: right to life, right to die, death penalty, homosexuality, pollution, energy, cancer and smoking. All appeared as election issues, and often in the form of referenda. The major social and political issues of the day involve questions concerning the relationship of society to biology. We still do not realize that man is a biological creature.

At the same time, psychology developed a major revolution in paradigms with the behaviorism of Watson and Skinner and the new biopsychological learning theories based on the neural sciences (Jeffery, 1977: Jeffery, 1978). Psychology and psychiatry are today based on biology and the biochemistry of the brain.

Today every behavioral and social science is finding its roots in biology, with the major opposition occurring in sociology. This movement is seen in biopolitics (Somit, 1976); in bioeconomics (Boulding, 1978: Gregory, et al. 1978); in anthropology (Laughlin and d'Aquili, 1974; Jorgensen, 1972; Katz, 1974; Stein and Rowe, 1974, Fox, 1975); and in sociology (van den Berghe, 1978; Ellis, 1977). Some of the biggest names in political science, economics, anthropology, psychology, and psychiatry are now involved in biological issues. Only sociology stands out as an opponent of biological systems.

All paradigmatic shifts (Kuhn, 1962) are accompanied by political revolutions and political opposition. Within the history of science we have witnessed the persecution of figures such as Newton, Galileo, and da Vinci for their scientific beliefs. We could add Madame Curie, Darwin, Veblen, and Semmelweiss. Semmelweiss was an Austrian physician who suggested that child-birth infections could be controlled by simple sanitation procedures such as washing one's hands. For this Semmelweiss was driven to an insane asylum. Servetus was burned at the stake by John Calvin for his studies of blood circulation (no doubt to balance the persecution of Galileo by the Catholic Church). Eleven of the recent Nobel Prize winners in science have been Jewish refugees from Nazi Germany.

Although some major breakthroughs have occurred in recent years in the biology of crime (Mednick and Christiansen, 1977; Hippchen, 1978; Lewis and Balla, 1976; Hare and Schalling, 1978; Feldman, 1977; Eysenck, 1977), it is still popular to label any reference to biology in criminology as "neo-Lombrosianism." At a recent meeting of the American Sociology Society, I presented a paper on genetics and criminology and was greeted as a Neo-Lombrosian who did not know that the field of genetics has nothing to do with behavior. At the 1978 meeting of the American Society of Criminology (ASC) the Norwegian recipient of the Sellin-Glueck award accepted his prize by denouncing the meeting as a futile attempt at neo-Lombrosian ideas. It is ironic that the name of Glueck is involved since Sheldon and Eleanor Glueck insisted for over thirty years on the importance of biological factors in criminality. The sense of scientific history is destroyed by the use of the phrase "neo-Lombrosian" since none of the biology of today was available to Lombroso—in fact, the biology of today was not around in 1950. Lombroso discussed phenotypic traits such as skull size and shape and length of arms, none of which are directly linked to behavior by our current knowledge of the brain. We can criticize Gall for measuring the bumps on the head, but at least we now know that those bumps have neural tissue underneath that do control behavior.

Thus the rejection of new ideas in science is not new. The reason for the opposition to and hatred of biology can be traced to basic assumptions about human nature. It is assumed that we possess free will; are free, moral, humanistic agents; have the equipotentiality for any behavior; and that if we are somehow determined, we are determined only by our social environment (Jeffery, 1978). The communist doctrine of Lamarkianism and environmental determinism destroyed the notion of genetic foundations of behavior and genetic differences among individuals. The other unfortunate political use of genetics was by the Nazis and the racists. The development of behaviorism by Skinner was also antigenetic; Skinner also insists on total environmental determinism. There is also in sociology the Durkheimian argument that social facts must exclude biology and psychology. The rejection of biology also represents a serious antiscientific movement which has—under the title of Marxian conflict theory—engulfed a great deal of criminology in recent years.

In the 1960s we witnessed a return to conflict theory in criminology. This movement has been referred to as "the new school of criminology" which, like the phrase "neo-Lombrosianism," implies no sense of history for those who use these phrases. Conflict theory is not new—in fact it is the oldest type of social philosophy. It is opposed to science and the use of science to understand man, and looks to the social and political structure for the answers to crime. This approach ignores the fact that conflict theory developed from Darwin's theory of evolution and natural selection. Marx cannot be understood unless one recognizes that he wrote at the same time and about the same topics as Darwin. Natural selection and survival for Darwin became class conflict for Marx. Adaptation to the environment for Darwin was materialism and technology for Marx. Marx was a social Darwinist, not in the sense the term was used in the early twentieth century, but in the sense that the two major issues in Darwin's theory of evolution were the two basic issues in Marxist ideology. It is popular in criminology today to refer to issues of law and crime as critical issues involving white collar crime, political crime, racism, sexism, and so forth, but without reference to the behavioral theory behind them. It is automatically assumed that if one is interested in political issues, one is not involved in biology or psychology. This ability of the investigator to separate the legal and ethical issues from the scientific issues is a major hangup in current criminological analysis. How can we discuss the behaviors of our politicians or our business leaders if we do not have a theory of behavior?

Another major development in criminology which has colored behavioral research was the rejection of liberal criminology in the late 1960s, and the acceptance of conservative criminology as a basis for political action. By liberal criminology we mean that policy originating with the positivists who taught that behavior could be studied and understood and criminals could be reformed and treated. The war on poverty would reduce delinquency through social engineering which dealt with poverty, unemployment, inadequate education, and racial discrimination. (Reckless and Allen, 1979; Finkenauer, 1978; Walker, 1978).

In 1964, Barry Goldwater made crime a major political issue under the banner of law and order. The conservative position originated with classical criminology and the theory of punishment and deterrence which lawyers and politicians have never given up. This position embraces the criminal justice system, the police, the courts, and corrections. It favors reversing the Warren Court and its liberal decisions on criminal justice. It presumes guilt, fixed sentences, and the use of prisons as a modern means of fighting crime. The conservative position is found in the writings of Martinson (Lipton et al. 1975) who found that rehabilitation was dead (see also Morris [1974]; Wilson [1975]; Fogel [1975]; van den Haag [1975]; and von Hirsch [1976] among others). We now have a serious movement on the part of state legislatures to increase prison sentences, and to make long sentences mandatory (Lagoy et al. 1978).

The conservative position has been joined by the deterrence and punishment philosophy which was revived by Isaac Errlich (1975) in his statistical argument that the execution of criminals reduces the crime rate. Executions are again with us to demonstrate to the world the contribution of criminology and the criminal justice system to the advancement of mankind, and to prove once again that Winston Churchill was right when he said a civilization is judged by the way it treats its prisoners.

The conservative position became official policy under the Johnson Administration with the President's Commission

and the Safe Streets Act (Reckless and Allen, 1979; Finkenauer, 1978; Walker, 1978). LEAA was created to put a law
and order philosophy into practice, and states were pushed
into this philosophy immediately by the attraction of federal
funding. It has been argued by a political scientist (Fiorina,
1977) that Congress is able to stay in power through this
distribution of the wealth by means of the federal tax program. In the case of crime control policy the federal tax
dollar destroyed any semblance of criminology as a behavioral science. Money was poured into the training of
police and court personnel, and university administrators
were quick to see the shift in Washington from funding of
basic research in the natural and behavioral sciences to
funding of vocational programs. Criminology programs were
ignored and criminal justice programs by the thousands
were developed in a span of a very few years.

When LEAA failed to reduce the crime rate through a
tough law and order position, a shift in policy occurred; im-
proving the quality of jusitice became the new official policy.
Nowhere in the LEAA structure—especially at the National
Institute—was systematic research on behavioral issues
carried out. The Institute managed to avoid the hard questions about crime and criminal behavior (White and Krislov,
1977). Under growing criticism from all sources, LEAA
underwent major reorganization under the Carter administration. However, at this time, the official policy seems to
be more of the same.

The man nominated by President Carter to head the new
LEAA (a conservative who advocates punishment in place of
behavioral research) was so seriously criticized for his
views on gun control and drug control that his name had to
be withdrawn. I opposed the pursuit of an LEAA policy
dominated by this position because I found it to be regres-
sive and destructive (Jeffery, 1978); however, the man
nominated to make policy for the federal government was
turned down by the Senate because his views were too
progressive.

Under a new regime, the National Institute has announced that some attention will be paid to criminal behavior and the causes of crime (Ewing, 1978). Support for longitudinal research, including genetic research, is now occurring. However, if this news ever reaches the general public it will receive a Golden Fleece of the month award.

For some time, federal policy has slighted or eliminated research and scientific efforts. This started with Richard Nixon as part of an anti-intellectual movement. The effort to kill basic behavioral research can be seen in three specific cases analyzed by the Institute of Society, Ethics, and the Life Sciences (1978). They are: (1) killing the Center for the Study of Violence at the University of California at Los Angeles; (2) killing research on the XYY abnormality at Harvard University; and (3) killing behavioral modification programs by LEAA. New restraints on human subject research, as well as limitations on funding, make research in the behavioral sciences almost impossible today.

It is ironic that in the 1970s, when biology and psychology are developing a greater understanding of human behavior, criminology is dominated by harsh punishment and nonresearch policy. Kittrie (1971) argued that we need a treatment system with legal safeguards. His book is often cited as evidence that treatment does not work and that we should return to a punitive approach. But he says quite clearly that emphasis on individual guilt and punishment is ironic and anachronistic. Rather, he favors a therapeutic approach to a punitive one (Kittrie, 1971: 405-407). Judge David Bazelon, the father of the Durham decision, noted in U.S. v. Alexander (1973) that if a therapy does not work, the law allows it; if the therapy works, the law does not allow its use.

We have three models of criminology and criminal justice in operation today. (1) A punishment/deterrence model based on conservative law and order politics. (2) A Marxian model based on social conflict which makes the politician the criminal and finds the solution to crime in social revolution. (3) A liberal social engineering model which believes in social determinism without any genetic or biological input into human behavior.

A fourth position has been put forth (Jeffery, 1977, Jeffery, 1978). It is a biosocial interdisciplinary model which argues that behavior can be scientifically understood and crime can be prevented rather than treated or punished. This model is a crime prevention model or a medical model of crime control. The psychiatrist Seymour Halleck supports the notion of individual biopsychological approaches to the treatment of criminal offenders. He argues that rehabilitation is not dead and he supports a humanistic, therapeutic approach to the rehabilitation of offenders (Halleck, 1975; Halleck and Witte, 1977).

We were fortunate at the 1978 ASC meeting to have a number of biologists, psychologists, and political scientists participating in the program. Mednick (1977) discussed the genetic foundations of antisocial behavior. Lewis (1976) discussed the role of brain damage and psychopathology in delinquency. Gordon (1976) updated his study of the relationship of low intelligence to delinquency. Horn, a behavioral geneticist from the University of Texas, discussed the general issue of genetics, intelligence, and criminal behavior. Hoffer (Hippchen, 1978) discussed the biochemical approaches to antisocial behavior. There was also a panel on nutrition, hypoglycemia, and learning disabilities, and a major plenary session on policy issues conducted by Gerhard Mueller (United Nations), Robert McKay (Aspen Institute), and Seymour Halleck.

The papers presented in the program represented a cross section of topics: genetics, brain function, learning disabilities, nutrition, violence, sociopathy, learning theory, and punishment. We are fortunate to have published here papers by several outstanding scholars from disciplines outside of sociology and criminology. Kenneth Moyer is a well-known psychologist working the area of violence and aggression. Seymour Halleck received the Sutherland award this year for his work in psychiatry and crime. Benson Ginsburg is a geneticist. Fred Kort is a political scientist who has joined with Ginsburg and others at the University of Connecticut to establish an interdisciplinary program in bio-politics. Maxson is a biologist and geneticist at the University of Connecticut.

I mentioned above that whenever criminologists discuss politics and law they immediately move into a different arena of analysis, that of social conflict and Marxian ideology. They forget that biology and psychology are critical to political analysis. There are, or course, ways other than Marxian to understand the state and legal systems. It is strange that the criminologist would not turn to the political scientist for help when he is interested in issues of this sort. The major issues raised today in political science are of a behavioral nature—or behavioralism as it is referred to in political science. As was mentioned above, some of the significant work in recent years has been in biopolitics. The criminologist/sociologist should therefore view the Kort-Maxson paper as an alternative to conflict theory and to the sociology of law as a means of understanding the political processes involved in the criminal justice system.

My first publication (Jeffery, 1956) dealt with the conflict between the crime and the criminal, the positivist v. the classical school. I asked how we could define crime by studying the individual offender, and I suggested a major effort be made to look at the political system as part of criminology. When one presents a topic such as biology and crime one is immediately confronted with such questions as: "how about political crimes and white collar crimes?" or "how about sexism and racism in the criminal justice system?" If it can be recognized that these questions are behavioral questions, and that the answers are to be found in biosocial analysis, then we can begin to find meaningful answers to such questions. When we point a finger at a politician, judge, police officer, or business executive we are asking essentially "why do human beings behave as they do?'' This volume is an attempt to throw some light on that issue.

My paper on the psychobiological aspects of punishment challenges the belief that punishment can be used successfully as a means of controlling human behavior. I point out that if we understand human behavior then we can better understand the behavior of our politicians. Punishment is used over and over again *not* because of its effect on the criminal, *but* because of its effect on those doing the punishing: lawyers, judges, attorney generals, governors, and the general public. People feel good when they execute others: why else would they continue to do it? Punishment is a biosocial act involving biology and the brain. Punishment is also basic to our educational, economic, and political systems. If we do not understand behavior, we do not understand politics.

I have referred to the political controversies surrounding biopolitics and sociobiology. If I may I would like to mention my good friend Fred Kort. Fred and I were senior fellows at the University of Chicago Law School. Since then he has moved, as have I, into the arena of biology and behavioral science. At public meetings where biopolitics was discussed he has been called a Fascist and Nazi. It is ironic to note that Fred Kort had to flee from Nazi Germany to preserve his life.

We are also fortunate to have outstanding articles in this volume by Dynes, Carlson, and Allen, by Holtzman, and by Kelly. These articles are a major breakthrough in the paper curtain which has so effectively isolated criminology from biology and psychology for so many years. If this is neo-Lombrosianism, so be it.

Finally it must be noted that our rejection of new knowledge about human behavior, at a time when we are burning people at the stake, creates an impossible moral dilemma. Today much of the opposition to sociobiology (Gregory et al., 1978; Caplan, 1978) is couched in moralistic and ethical terms. It is assumed that humanistic man cannot coexist with scientific man. The present state of world affairs suggests that perhaps we had better join the two. We have examples of an emerging bioethics, as found in The Self and Its Brain by Karl Popper (1977), a philosopher and historian, and John Eccles, a brain scientist. Another example is The Biological Origin of Human Values by George Pugh (1977). The ethical and social systems that appear in the Bible or in Plato's Republic, and are part of man's history, were originally a product of genetic evolution and the human brain. We cannot separate man's ethical and social systems from his brain and biological system.

REFERENCES

BOULDING, K. E. (1978) Ecodynamics. Beverly Hills, CA: Sage.

CAPLAN, A. L. (1978) The Sociobiology Debate. New York: Harper & Row.

ELLIS, L. (1977) "The decline and fall of sociology: 1975-2000." Amer. Sociologist 12 (May): 56-66.

EHRLICH, I. (1975) "The deterrent effect of capital punishment: a question of life and death." Am. Econ. Rev. 65: 397-417.

EWING, B. G. (1978) National Institute of Law Enforcement and Criminal Justice Program Plan: 1979. Washington, DC: National Institute of Law Enforcement and Criminal Justice.

EYSENCK, H. (1977) Crime and Personality. London: Routledge & Kegan Paul.

FELDMAN, M. P. (1977) Criminal Behaviour. New York: John Wiley.

FINCKENAUER, J. O. (1978) "Crime as a National Political Issue: 1964-76" Crime and Delinquency 24 (January): 13-27.

FIORINA, M. P. (1977) Congress: Keystone of the Washington Establishment. New Haven, CT: Yale Univ. Press.

FOGEL, D. (1975) We are the Living Proof. Cincinnati: Anderson.

FOX, R. (1975) Biological Anthropology. New York: John Wiley.

GREGORY, M. S., A. SILVERS, and D. SUTCH (1978) Sociobiology and Human Nature. San Francisco: Jossey-Bass.

GORDON, R. (1976). "Prevalence: the rare datum in delinquency." In Malcolm Klein (ed.) The Juvenile Justice System. Beverly Hills, CA: Sage.

HALLECK, S. et al. [eds.] (1975) The Aldine Criminal Justice Annual: 1974. Chicago: Aldine.

——— and A. WITTE (1977) "Is rehabilitation dead?" Crime and Delinquency 23 (October): 372-382.

HARE, R. D. and D. SCHALLING (1978) Psychopathic Behavior. New York: John Wiley.

HIPPCHEN, L. (1978) Ecologic-Biochemical Approaches to Treatment of Delinquents and Criminals. New York: Van Nostrand Reinhold.

Institute of Society, Ethics, and Life Sciences (1978) The Dynamics of Scientific Research: Three Case Studies of Scientific Research on Aggression. Hastings-on-Hudson: Hastings Center.

JEFFERY, C. R. (1978) "Criminology as an interdisciplinary behavioral science." Criminology 16 (August): 149-169.

——— (1977) Crime Prevention Through Environmental Design. Beverly Hills, CA: Sage.

——— (1956) "The structure of criminological thinking." J. of Criminal Law, Criminology and Police Sci. 46 (January-February): 658-672.

JORGENSEN, J. (1972) Biology and Culture in Modern Perspective. San Francisco: W. H. Freeman.

KATZ, S. (1974) Biological Anthropology. San Francisco: W. H. Freeman.

KITTRIE, N. (1971) The Right to be Different. Baltimore: Johns Hopkins Univ. Press.

KUHN, T. (1962) The Structure of Scientific Revolution. Chicago: Univ. of Chicago Press.

LAGOY, S. P., F. A. HUSSEY, and J. H. KRAMER (1978) "A comparative assessment of determinate sentencing in the four pioneer states." Crime and Delinquency 24 (October): 385-400.

LAUGHLIN, C. D. and E. C. D'AQUILI (1974) Biogenetic Structuralism. New York: Columbia Univ. Press.

LEWIS, D. O. and D. A. BALLA (1976) Delinquency and Psychopathology. New York: Grune and Stratton.

LIPTON, D., R. MARTINSON, and J. WILKS (1975) Effectiveness of Correctional Treatment. New York: Praeger.

MEDNICK, S. and K. O. CHRISTIANSEN (1977) Biosocial Bases of Criminal Behavior. New York: Gardner.

MORRIS, N. (1974) The Future of Imprisonment. Chicago: Univ. of Chicago Press.

POPPER, K. R. and J. C. ECCLES (1977) The Self and its Brain. London: Springer International.

PUGH, G. E. (1977) The Biological Origins of Human Values. New York: Basic Books.

RECKLESS, W. C. and H. E. ALLEN (1979) "Developing a national crime policy: impact of politics on crime in America." In Criminology: *New Concerns and New Directions,* ed. by Edward Sagarin. Beverly Hills: Sage.

SOMIT, A. (1976) Biology and Politics: Recent Explorations. Hawthorne, NY: Mouton.

STEIN, P. and B. M. ROWE (1974) Physical Anthropology. New York: McGraw Hill.

U.S. v. ALEXANDER (1973) 471 F. 2nd 964.

VAN DEN BERGHE, P. L. (1978) Man in Society: A Biosocial View. New York: Elsevier.

VAN DEN HAAG (1975) Concerning Punishing Criminals. New York: Basic Books.

VON HIRSCH, A. (1976) Doing Justice: The Choice of Punishments. New York: Hill & Wang.

WALKER, S. (1978) "Reexamining the President's Crime Commission: the challenge of crime in a free society after ten years." Crime and Delinquency 24 (January): 1-12.

WHITE, S. O. and S. KRISLOV (1977) Understanding Crime. Washington, DC.: National Academy of Sciences.

WILSON, J. Q. (1975) Thinking About Crime. New York: Basic Books.

Kenneth Moyer
Carnegie-Mellon University

2

WHAT IS THE POTENTIAL FOR BIOLOGICAL VIOLENCE CONTROL?

INTRODUCTION

In meetings on criminology that I have attended recently, there has been considerable concern about and discussion of the organic bases of criminal behavior. I would like to direct my remarks to two different aspects of that problem.

It is, of course, true that all criminal behavior, like all other behavior, has an organic or a physiological basis. Behavior is controlled by the brain which reflects the individual's past experience. A mother's love, a father's scorn, punishment, reward, and solitary confinement in a prison all have an effect, and a relatively permanent one on the brain. When we teach a child to say "Please may I have a cookie," instead of "Hey you, gimme a cookie," we are making relatively permanent changes in his brain, which are going to determine his behavior. When a child is rewarded for hitting another child to get what he wants, his brain is also changed. This kind of aggressive behavior— that used to gain specific ends—is frequently referred to as instrumental aggression, and we will say more about it later.

These changes occur, in general, in the cerebral cortex and involve primarily the neural processes concerned with learning. These are the kinds of brain mechanisms that may help determine whether an individual will tend to emulate General Patton or St. Francis of Assisi. They are probably not the primary mechanisms which might turn him into a Charles Whitman.

There are processes in other parts of the brain that contribute to and help to determine other types of behavior. When certain neural systems in the lower brain are active, one has an internal sensation of hunger and the probability of eating behavior is increased. When other neural systems in that portion of the brain are active, feelings associated with sexual responses are reported. There are also neural systems in the lower brain which result in feelings of anger or irritability. When they are active the result is that the probability of aggressive behavior is increased.

I have suggested a dichotomy between the two parts of the brain, cerebral cortex, and the lower portion. It must be pointed out that such a distinction is drawn only with the license of the lecturer: to clarify, to highlight and to promote understanding of the different kinds of mechanisms. Actually, the different levels and different parts and systems of the brain always interact to determine behavior. The brain processes that control learning and memory are constantly interacting with those processes that control basic motivational and feeling processes. However, the distinction is a useful one for the purposes of discussion.

Our concern will be with the second mechanism which is largely responsible for certain types of crime, that is, aggressive, destructive, or violent behavior. More is known about these brain processes and we now have some idea about how to alter their functioning. A model will be presented that will provide some of the details on the underlying mechanisms for crimes of this nature. I will also cover the potential for altering these brain mechanisms and suggest ways in which such alterations might contribute to the control of this kind of aggression. Finally, we will consider the limitations of the physiological approaches to criminal behavior.

It should be pointed out first that aggression is not a unitary construct. There are a number of different kinds of aggressive behavior (Moyer, 1968). This means that it is impossible to construct a single model that will fit all of them in detail. However, we can deal with the mechanisms or the kinds of mechanisms that are common to some if not most of the different kinds of aggressive behavior. The basic premise of this model is that there are, in the brains of animals and humans, neural systems that, when fired in the presence of a relevant target, result in aggressive or destructive behavior towards that target. In the case of humans, the actual aggressive behavior may be controlled, but the individual will have the appropriate feelings of hostility. There is now abundant evidence to support that premise.

NEURAL SYSTEMS FOR AGGRESSION

Some of the most fundamental work in this area has been done by John Flynn at Yale. He has worked with cats and has enlarged on techniques that were developed in the early 1940s. It is possible to implant an electrode in specific areas deep in an animal's brain. The electrode can then be attached to a plug that is cemented to the skull. The plug can then be attached to a stimulation source and it is possible to stimulate the depths of the brain of an animal that is awake and free to move around. When the experiment is finished for the day, the subject can be returned to its home cage none the worse for the experience.

The cats used by Flynn were nonpredatory and would not normally attack rats. Some, in fact, would live with a rat for months and not molest it. If an electrode implanted in the cat's lateral hypothalamus is electrically activated, the animal will ignore the experimenter, but will immediately attack and kill an available rat. The kill will be quite precise: a bite in the cervical region of the spinal cord in the typical predatory behavior of the feline. However, if the electrode is located in the medial hypothalamus, and the cat is stimulated in the presence of the rat, it will ignore the rat and attack the experimenter. The attack on the experimenter will be highly directed. It is not similar to the random attacks of a decerebrate animal. This cat appears as though it intends to do the experimenter harm, and in fact, it will (Egger and Flynn, 1963).

One particularly interesting experiment that illustrates a number of things, was done by Robinson and his colleagues (Robinson et al., 1969). They took a small Rhesus monkey and implanted an electrode in the anterior hypothalamus. They then put the animal in a primate chair, activated the electrode, and showed that the monkey did not become aggressive towards inanimate objects, nor did it become aggressive towards the experimenter. It was then put in a cage with another monkey that was larger and more dominant than the experimental animal, and with the dominant monkey's female consort. When stimulated in this situation the experimental monkey vigorously and immediately attacked the dominant monkey. It did not attack the female. It attacked only the dominant male monkey. This appeared to be a valid primate attack because the dominant monkey reacted by counterattacking just as viciously as it usually would if attacked by a submissive animal. This scenario was repeated a number of times and although the result is quite unusual, the Robinson group found that the dominance relationship changed. The stimulation-induced attacks were so intense that the formerly dominant animal ultimately became submissive to the experimental monkey.

This experiment shows first that the particular brain stimulation used resulted in one specific kind of aggression, which I have called "inter-male," that is, the specific tendency for one male to attack another. Second, this experiment demonstrates that aggressive behavior is stimulus bound. In the absence of the relevant stimulus, that monkey, even though stimulated time and again, showed no irritability or increased tendency to attack other targets. The essential results of these experiments have been repeated in many laboratories.

It is important not to generalize too quickly from one species to another. One must be particularly cautious in generalizing from animals to man. However, we now have good evidence that man, for all of his encephalization, has not escaped from the neural determinants of his aggressive behavior. There are now several hundred people who have electrodes implanted in their brains. The wires are attached to small sockets cemented to the skull. These patients can be brought into the laboratory, plugged in, and precise areas deep in the brain can be electrically stimulated.

A case reported by King (1961) is particularly instructive. This patient was a very mild-mannered woman who was a generally submissive, kind, and friendly person. An electrode was implanted in the area of her brain called the amygdala. Dr. King stimulated this pateint in the amygdala with a current of four milliamperes and there was no observable change in her behavior. (One cannot tell when one's brain is stimulated, there are no receptors that can indicate it, thus, she was unaware of the stimulation.) When the amperage was increased to five milliamperes, she became hostile and aggressive. She said such things as "Take my blood pressure. Take it now." Then she said, "If you're going to hold me you'd better get five more men." Whereupon she stood up and started to strike the experimenter. He then wisely turned down the current.

It was possible to turn this woman's anger on and off with a simple flick of the switch because the electrode was located in a part of the neural system for hostility. She indicated having felt anger. She also reported being concerned about the fact that she was angry. She did not report pain or other discomfort. She was simply "turned on" angry. Similar findings have been reported by other investigators (Sem-Jacobsen, 1968; Heath, 1954).

Brain Dysfunctions Relating to Aggression

There are a number of pathological processes in the human brain which result in the activation of the neural systems for feelings of hostility. Tumors with an irritative focus frequently result in increased irritability and rage attacks if they are located in particular portions of the brain. It is important to note that all brain tumors do not produce pathological aggression. Many, in fact, produce apathy and somnolence. However, if they develop in such a way as to impinge on and activate the neural systems for aggressive behavior, the syndrome of pathological aggressivity may appear. Tumors in the septal region, the temporal lobe, and the frontal lobe have produced this reaction. In 1962, Sano reported on 1800 cases of brain tumor and found the irritability syndrome in those that involved the temporal lobe and the anterior hypothalamus.

The literature contains many cases of pathological aggressiveness induced by brain tumors. Only a few examples are cited. Two violent patients with tumors of the temporal lobe are described by Sweet et al. (1969). One man, a powerful individual, attempted to kill his wife and daughter with a butcher knife. When brought to the hospital, he was in a full-blown rage reaction, during which he snarled, showed his teeth, and attempted to hit or kick anyone who came close enough. His history revealed that over a period of six months, his personality had gradually changed and that he had complained of blurred vision and intense headaches. When the tumor pressing on the anterior temporal lobe was removed, his symptoms rapidly abated.

Another patient who had shown hyperirritability for years began to show serious destructive rages. He drove his car recklessly and began to direct his outbursts of rage against his wife and son. Although intellectually capable as a chemist, he was unable to hold a position for longer than a few months because of his volatile and irritable behavior patterns. After the removal of a slow-growing tumor that had evidently been invading the temporal lobe over a period of several years, his symptoms disappeared. He became more stable, more placid, and functioned adequately as a chemist during the nineteen-month follow-up.

There are a variety of disorders that involve generalized damage to the central nervous system, including cerebral arteriosclerosis, senile dementia, Korsakoff's syndrome, and Huntington's chorea. These dysfunctions frequently present a common symptomatology referred to as chronic brain syndrome which is characterized by memory deficit, orientation loss, and affective disturbances. There are wide fluctuations of mood and a general emotional instability, but the affective pattern is dominated by anger, rage, and increased irritability (Lyght, 1966).

Epilepsy

Another neurological disorder which may result in an increase in aggressive tendencies is epilepsy, particularly temporal lobe epilepsy. It is certainly true that temporal lobe epilepsy is not necessarily accompanied by an increased tendency to impulsiveness and hostility, but the evidence indicates that the probability is increased.

Ictal aggression (that occuring during the seizure) is relatively rare. However, there is abundant evidence that uncontrolled, impulsive, assaultive behavior is not uncommon as an interictal behavior pattern, particularly among temporal lobe epileptics (Gastaut, 1954). Falconer et al. (1958) reporting on fifty patients, indicated that 38% of them showed spontaneous outbursts of aggression. About half of the psychomotor epileptic patients studied by Schwab et al. (1965) developed destructive behavior and paroxysmal bursts of anger as a part of a behavior disorder. Other investigators have reported similar results. (See Walker and Blumer, 1972; Serafetinides, 1970; Glaser et al., 1963.)

It is important to emphasize that the subjects in the preceding studies were from a highly selected population of individuals with epilepsy. They were, in general, people who had been committed to an institution or who were candidates for surgery. There are, of course, thousands of epileptics who are making an adequate adjustment in the real world and do not suffer from personality disturbances, impulsiveness, or uncontrolled, aggressive tendencies. Behavior pathology occurs only when certain specific neural systems are involved.

There is also evidence from several sources that, like many other systems in the brain, there are suppressor systems which are antagonistic to the aggression systems. Bernstein and I (Bernstein and Moyer, 1970) showed several years ago that if you remove the olfactory bulbs from a rat you turn a peaceful laboratory rat into a vicious animal that will attack other rats, mice, or the experimenter.

Wheatley (1944) showed many years ago that if the medial hypothalamus of the cat is lesioned, a tame cat is turned into a wild cat. It appears that these suppressor systems inhibit the activity in the neural systems for aggression. It should be pointed out that lesion experiments by themselves are not conclusive evidence of suppressor activity. However, much additional evidence for aggression suppressor systems is available and will be discussed later.

THRESHOLDS FOR AGGRESSION

It is fortunate that in neither humans nor animals is aggression very frequent. It is relatively uncommon. Thus, in order to understand the physiology of aggression, we must understand what it is that turns on these neural systems and what it is that turns them off. Perhaps one of the best ways to think about this is in terms of thresholds for the systems. In certain circumstances the threshold for firing the neural systems for aggression is very high. in that case it takes a great deal of provocation to activate them. There are other circumstances in which the threshold is very low and relatively little provocation will result in activating the neural systems with the result that the individual has an increased tendency to behave aggresively.

Hereditary Factors and Aggression Thresholds

Some of the variables that influence the thresholds of the neural systems for aggression appear to be hereditary. For example, we have shown in my laboratory that some strains of rats behave aggressively toward small chickens in significantly greater numbers than do other strains (Bandler and Moyer, 1970).

It is also possible, as Dr. Lagerspetz of Finland (1964) has shown, to take a large population of mice and select from them the aggressive and nonaggressive animals. Within a relatively few generations, if the very aggressive animals are mated, it is possible to develop a highly aggressive strain in which mice will attack immediately when they are put together. If the nonaggressive animals are bred, a strain can be developed that will not fight no matter what is done to them.

Dr. Wolpy at Earlham College in Indiana tells me that he is raising an extremely aggressive strain of rabbits. These rabbits will attack other rabbits or the experimenter. If some of these animals escape to the Indiana countryside, there are going to be some surprised hunting dogs. Obviously, we do not have any comparable data on human beings. However, if this model has any validity and if there are specific neural systems for different kinds of aggressive behavior, it must be that different thresholds for aggression are inherited. Neurological differences must be inherited in the same way that differences in the shapes of noses are.

Blood Chemistry Influences on Aggression

Another significant variable which contributes to differences in the aggression threshold level is blood chemistry. It has been known for centuries, of course, that one can take a raging bull and convert it into a gentle steer by the operation of castration which reduces the level of testosterone in the blood stream. The formal work on this problem was done in 1947 by Elizabeth Beeman, and has been repeatedly confirmed in many laboratories. Dr. Beeman worked with a strain of mice that would fight when put together. She castrated the animals of the experimental group prior to puberty. After maturity when those mice were put together they did not fight at all. The control group showed the usual amount of aggression characteristic of that strain. She then carried the experiment a step further and implanted pellets of testosterone subcutaneously in the castrated mice. When the testosterone became effective they fought at the same level as the control animals had. She then surgically removed the pellets of testosterone whereupon the mice once again became docile. It was possible to manipulate the aggressive behavior of these mice simply by changing the testosterone level.

There are a variety of other blood chemistry changes that influence the thresholds for aggression. For example, we know that frustration and stress are important variables in inducing aggressive behavior, particularly if the frustration and stress are prolonged. It seems likely that this occurs because the stressors change the hormonal status and thus change the thresholds of the neural systems for aggression. Although we do not yet have experimental evidence to support this conjecture, there are a number of people working on the problem.

It is also true, as many women have found, that there is a period during the week before menstruation when a significant percentage of women feel irritable, hostile, and are easily aroused to anger (Dalton, 1959, 1960, 1961, and 1964). Those who have had inadequate training in impulse control sometimes behave and act on those impulses. In fact, one study which was conducted on 249 female prison inmates showed that 62% of the crimes of violence were committed in the premenstrual week, whereas only 2% of the crimes of violence were committed in the postmenstrual week (Morton et al., 1953).

Lest anyone suggest that women's rights should in some way be restricted because of their periodic tendency to hostility, let me point out that from mouse to man, with very few exceptions, the male is the more aggressive sex. Recent statistics show that the homicide rate is five times as great for the male and for armed robbery it is about twenty times as great.

As Broom and Selznick (1957) said, "Compared with females, males have a greater excess of crimes in all nations, all communities within nations, all age groups, all periods of history for which we have statistics, and for all types of crime except those related to the female sex, such as abortion."

There appears to be good clinical evidence that a limited number of individuals show an irritable aggression reaction when their blood chemistry is altered by a sudden drop in blood sugar. This is the state of hypoglycemia. At least one controlled study supports the clinical findings. Dr. Ralph Bolton (1973) spent considerable time with a very hostile tribe of Peruvian indians, called the Qolla. He hypothesized that the exceptionally high level of social conflict and hostility in the society could be partly explained by the tendency to hypoglycemia among the community residents.

Peer ratings of aggressiveness (which had an acceptable reliability) were studied in relationship to blood sugar levels as determined by a four-hour glucose tolerance test. The aggression ratings were not known to the individuals who read the glucose levels. A Chi Square analysis of the data showed a statistically significant relationship between aggression ranking and the change in blood glucose levels during the test. In view of all of the other possible causes of aggressive behavior, this is a remarkable finding and indicates that the relationship must be a powerful one.

Allergies and Aggression

Another change in the blood chemistry which can result in irritability and hostile tendencies is that produced by certain allergens in some particularly susceptible people. The term "allergic tension-fatigue syndrome" was introduced in 1954 to describe the allergic behavior pattern (Speer, 1954). It is important to note that behavior disturbances are only one of many possible allergic reactions and that not everyone with allergies shows a behavioral alteration.

A classification of allergic reactions in the nervous system includes the following:

Emotional Immaturity Reactions: Included under this heading are temper tantrums, screaming episodes, whining, impatience, and excitability. Patients of this type are inclined to be erratic, impulsive, quarrelsome, and irresponsible. Many admit to having "childish" compulsions.

Antisocial Behavior: These patients are inclined to be uncooperative, pugnacious, sulky, and perhaps cruel. Most have learned enough self control to avoid serious abberations of behavior [Campbell, 1970: 31].

It is difficult to determine how extensive a problem allergic aggression is. There are relatively few studies comparing aggressive tendencies in allergic individuals with control subjects. And since it is clear that all allergic individuals do not have nervous system involvement, such studies would not be particularly meaningful. Although there are a large number of case studies in the literature showing that individuals with allergic tension-fatigue syndrome lose that symptomatology under allergy management, the only reasonable way to determine whether the syndrome is an allergic one is to eliminate the allergen from the environment until the symptoms abate and then reproduce the symptoms by reintroducing the allergen into the environment—the so-called challenge technique. Crook et al. (1961) reported on fifty patients who had five signs and symptoms of allergy: fatigue, irritability and other mental and emotional symptoms, pallor, circles under the eyes, and nasal congestion. The majority of the patients in this study had their symptoms relieved and reproduced by the challenge technique. The fifty patients reviewed in this research were seen in the group pediatric practice during a four-year period. The authors concluded that allergy as a systemic or generalized illness is much more common than is usually recognized by most allergy textbooks.

Allergens that can reproduce the allergic tension-fatigue syndrome are highly varied. It can be produced by pollens (Kahn, 1927); a variety of inhalants (Eisenberg, 1970; Randolph, 1962); drugs (Gottlieb, 1970a; Schaffer, 1953); and many foods, of which milk, chocolate, cola, corn, and eggs are the most common (Speer, 1970; Crook et al., 1961). The sensitivity of the individual varies idiosyncratically and according to the type of allergen. One patient showed such exquisite sensitivity to onions that she could tell when they were being cooked, not by the odor but because she had a sudden and intense nervousness and irritability (Frederichs and Goodman, 1969).

The basic physiological cause of the irritable allergic reaction is not yet clear. Perhaps the most reasonable hypothesis is suggested by Gottlieb (1970b), who considers the possibility that the symptoms are due to allergically caused circumscribed angioedema (noninflammatory swelling) of the brain. There is some evidence that such localized edema occurs in the brain as a result of allergies just as localized edema occurs in the skin. Both types of edema are reversible. As with the skin, there is evidence that the edema may be localized in different parts of the brain. Thus the number and kinds of symptoms will be a function of the particular location of the resultant pressure in the brain. If the angioedema occurs in any one of several portions of the brain through which the neural system for irritable aggression courses, the pressure of the swelling may sensitize or activate those neural systems with the resultant feeling of hostility or aggressive behavior.

AGGRESSION CONTROL

It is probably true that most of the time for most crimes, the most relevant variables are social, sociological, and cultural. In the broad meaning of the term, they are the result of learned reactions. They come from changes in the brain which occur in the cortex and are the result of experience. Thus, there can be no doubt that some of the most important methods for the control of criminal and anti-social behavior involve retraining, reeducation, and social changes. That is, the external environment is manipulated in some way to alter the individual's behavior or his potential for socially unacceptable behavior. However, if this model has any validity, it should be possible to change certain kinds of aggressive behavior by influencing the internal milieu, by producing changes in the individual's physiology.

I should emphasize at this point that what is possible is certainly not necessarily desirable. I shall discuss what is possible and later will consider some of the implications of those possibilities.

Brain Lesions and Aggression Control

If there are neural systems which are active during and responsible for aggressive behavior it should be possible to reduce or eliminate aggressive tendencies by interrupting or interfering with those neural systems. There is now abundant evidence that such a procedure is possible. As might be suspected when dealing with neural systems rather than neural centers, there are a number of different brain areas which may be lesioned to delimit aggressive tendencies.

One can take the wild cat *Lynx rufus rufus* which will attack with the slightest provocation, and make it tame by burning out a very small part of the brain called the amygdala. After the operation it will never be violent again (Schreiner and Kling, 1953).

The same thing can be done with the wild Norway rat, one of the few animals which will attack without apparent provocation. If a bilateral amygdalectomy is done on this animal, as soon as it comes out of the anesthetic, it will become docile. You can pick it up and carry it around in your lab coat pocket (Woods, 1956).

Just as there are wild cats and wild monkeys, there are wild people, individuals who have so much spontaneous activity in the neural systems which underlie aggressive behavior that they are a constant threat to themselves and to those around them. They are confined to the back wards of mental hospitals under constant sedation or restraint. The homicidal hostility of these persons can also be reduced if appropriate brain lesions are made to interrupt the functioning of the systems for irascibility.

There are a number of surgeons now who have done essentially the same operation on humans as described above for the cat and the rat. That is, a complete or partial bilateral amygdalectomy. The Japanese investigator Narabayashi and his colleagues for example, indicate that they obtained 85% success in the reduction of violent behavior after a bilateral amygdalectomy (Narabayashi et al., 1963). Dr. Heimburger in Indiana claims that he obtains 92% increase in docility in these extremely violent patients through the same operation. Not only was it possible to put those individuals in the open wards, that is take them out of isolation, but two of his patients have been released into society and are making at least a reasonable adjustment (Heimburger et al., 1966).

There can be no doubt that a number of different brain lesions can reduce the tendency of an individual to both feel and express hostility. The fact is of considerable theoretical significance. It confirms many of the findings on animals and substantiates predictions from the model described above. However, as a practical therapy for the control of aggressive behavior, it leaves much to be desired. There are very few individuals for whom such a drastic approach would be indicated. The most serious problem with the use of lesions for the control of aggression is that the operation is not reversible. Once the lesion is made, nothing can be done to restore the individual to the preoperative state. When the operation is not successful, and it sometimes is not, the patient is brain damaged to no avail. It therefore appears clear that surgery should be a last resort therapy and should be used only after all other types of control, both psychological and physiological, have been tried. There is evidence that in some of the hospitals around the world in which aggression control operations are performed, relatively little care is taken to ensure that brain surgery is, indeed, the "last resort therapy" that it should be.

Brain Stimulation and Aggression Control

The control of aggressive behavior can also be achieved by the activation of those neural systems which send inhibitory fibers to the aggression systems. Delgado has repeatedly shown that vicious rhesus monkeys can be tamed by the stimulation of aggression suppressor areas.

To eliminate the need for restraint and the necessity for connecting wires to the head, a technique was developed by which the brain of the subject could be stimulated by remote, radio control. The monkey wore a small stimulating device on its back which was connected by leads under the skin to the electrodes which were implanted in various locations in the brain. The leads were connected through a very small switching relay which could be closed by an impulse from a miniature radio receiver which was bolted to the animal's skull. The radio receiver could then be activated by a transmitter which was some distance away. With this system it was possible to study the monkeys while permitting them to roam free in the caged area (Delgado, 1963).

In one experiment the subject was the aggressive boss monkey which dominated the rest of the colony with his threatening behavior and overt attacks. A radio controlled electrode was implanted in the monkey's caudate nucleus. When the radio transmitter was activated the boss monkey received stimulation in the caudate nucleus with the result that his spontaneous aggressive tendencies were blocked. His territoriality diminished and the other monkeys in the colony reacted to him differently. They made fewer submissive gestures and showed less fear of the boss. When the caudate nucleus was being stimulated, it was possible for the experimenter to enter the cage and catch the monkey with his bare hands.

During one phase of the experiment described above, the button for the transmitter was placed inside the cage near the feeding tray and thus made available to all of the monkeys in the colony. One small monkey learned to stand next to the button and watch the boss monkey. Every time the boss would start to threaten and become aggressive the little monkey would push the button and calm him down. I leave it to the reader to decide what the political implications of this experiment are. I must say that it is perhaps the first experimental evidence of St. Matthew's prediction that the meek shall indeed inherit the earth.

Man also has neural systems in the brain which, when activated, function to block ongoing aggressive behavior. Dr. Heath from Tulane has reported on a patient who had an electrode implanted in an area of the brain called the septum. This extremely hostile patient would be brought into the room raging, threatening, swearing, and struggling. When his electrode was connected and the septal region was stimulated (without his knowledge, of course) he immediately relaxed, became docile, and assumed a positive attitude. Further, he was unable to account for the sudden change in his behavior. When the stimulating electrode is in the septal area, the patient may tell a dirty joke or reveal plans to seduce the waitress down at the corner bar (Heath, 1954). There are other suppressor areas, however, that do not activate sexually toned responses.

It would be possible to run the wire from that electrode down the back of this patient's neck to a battery pack that he could wear on his belt. You could then give him an "anti-hostility button" and whenever he began to feel very mean he could press the button, calm himself down, and rejoin the civilized world.

The technology has already been developed. Heath developed it as a therapeutic device for an individual with narcolepsy (Heath, 1954). Narcolepsy, as you probably know, is a disorder in which the individual falls asleep at inappropriate times (I have had many students afflicted with this disorder). This particular patient suggested that his narcolepsy was very troublesome because it interfered with his profession. He was a night club entertainer and would sometimes fall asleep in the middle of his act. What Dr. Heath did was to implant an electrode in the arousal system of the brain. A wire was then brought down to a transistorized stimulation unit and the patient was given an "on button." Whenever he started to drift off to sleep the patient could press his "on button" and turn himself back on. He had a type of narcolepsy in which he sometimes fell asleep before he could get to the button. His friends soon learned, however, that when he did that they could reach over and press his "on button" and bring him back into the conversation.

I pointed out that Delgado had his monkey hooked up to a radio. There is no reason why exactly the same technique could not be used on humans. At least four people have been reported in the literature to have been under radio control of one sort or another (Delgado et al., 1968). An electrode could be placed in a suppressor area of the brain just as Delgado did with the boss monkey. It could be brought out to a radio which is bolted to the subject's head. His brain could then be activated by a transmitter and the patient could then range as widely as the area that the transmitter reached.

There are of course some problems with this approach. Since the radio has to be bolted to the skull, it means that the bolts have to go through the scalp. This is a constant possible source of irritation, and a source of infection. There are also psychological problems. People tend to report that they feel conspicuous with radios on their heads.

But even those problems are being solved by the recent developments in microminiaturization in electronics. It is now possible to take the radio, the power to operate it, and a radio transmitter which will send out brain waves and put them all into a unit which is about the size and the shape of a half dollar. The electrode can be put in place, and attached to this unit which can be implanted anywhere under the skin. As soon as the individual's hair grows back he looks like anyone else. In fact, it is technologically possible right now that the next person you meet on the street will be under radio control and you would not know it unless he parted his hair wrong that morning.

The suppression of aggression by electrical stimulation is, I think, of considerable theoretical importance. We know that humans possess these neural suppressor systems and we are gradually learning many of the characteristics of suppression mechanisms. However, like brain lesions, this is not yet a reasonable or a useful therapeutic technique

The surgical risk of mortality through electrode implants is even lower than that of stereotaxic brain lesions; it can, in fact, be considered negligible. But there are other serious side effects which merit a great deal more research before electrical stimulation of human brains can be considered risk free. Although there are no data on humans, it has been shown in mice, rats, cats, and monkeys that repeated, brief, subthreshold stimulation of the amygdala results in a progressive lowering of the seizure threshold and ultimately in behavioral convulsions. This increase in seizure potential resulting from brain stimulation has been referred to as the kindling effect. Goddard (1972), who has studied this phenomenon in some detail, concludes that the kindling effect is a relatively permanent transynaptic change resulting from the stimulation. It is not due to tissue damage or scar formation.

It may someday be possible to circumvent the kindling effects. Until then, however, any procedure which involves repeated electrical stimulation of the human brain places the patient at risk.

Hormonal Control of Aggression

Our physiological model of aggressive behavior indicates that the neurological systems for aggressive behavior are sensitized by chemicals in the blood stream. These are primarily, but not exclusively, hormones. An understanding of the endocrinology and blood chemistry influences on aggression should ultimately lead to a rational therapy for certain kinds of hostility in humans. The woman, for example, who suffers from periodic hyper-irritability every month has a physician who either isn't aware of the problem or doesn't keep up on the literature. There are a variety of therapeutic measures now which can be taken to alleviate that problem.

There are also people who show a kind of aggressive behavior, known as sex-related aggression. These are the violent individuals for whom the object of aggression is the same as the object for sexual behavior. These are the men who commit brutal sex murders.

Aggressive behavior which is directly associated with sexual behavior, either heterosexual or homosexual, can sometimes be controlled by reducing or blocking the androgens in the blood stream. The simplest and most obvious method of accomplishing this is through the operation of castration. There is now considerable evidence that this operative procedure is effective in reducing the level of sexual arousal regardless of its direction. This is a drastic therapy and there are obvious problems with it. It is permanent and irreversible. There are also a variety of physical and psychological side effects. However, it has been offered to sex criminals as an alternative to prison in some countries (Bremer, 1959).

More recently some investigators have attempted to block the effects of the male hormone by giving estrogenic or progestogenic hormones or antiandrogenic drugs. Although a great deal more work needs to be done and the problem of side effects must be considered, these techniques do show promise (Chatz, 1972; Blumer and Migeon, 1973).

Pharmaceutical Control of Aggression

The activity of the neural systems responsible for aggressive behavior and feelings of hostility can also be reduced by the use of drugs. Although there is currently no drug which is a completely specific antihostility agent, there are available a significant number of preparations which do reduce aggressive tendencies as one component of their action. However, the problem of predicting which drug will be effective in the inhibition of hostility in a given individual is a difficult problem. Aggressive behavior has many causes and can result from a variety of neural and endocrine dysfunctions. There are not, as yet, good diagnostic tests which permit a rational pharmacotherapeutic approach to hostility control. However, in spite of this lack of a perfect predictability in matching a specific drug to a particular patient, there are now a large number of substances which are useful in the management of aggression. It is already possible to reduce or eliminate much of the irrational, nonadaptive hostility found in psychotic, neurotic, and ostensibly normal individuals.

Time does not permit a review of the extensive literature on the pharmacological control of aggression. However, it should be indicated that most of the major tranquilizers such as chlorpromazine appear to have an antihostility effect over and above their sedative action. This also appears to be true of many of the minor tranquilizers including librium and valium. There are many other pharmaceutical agents which have a taming effect, but none of them works on all patients, and some may even exacerbate the hostile tendencies in some patients. Until more precise diagnostic procedures are available, the simple dictum for treatment will remain; if the first drug on the list does not work, try the next one. (See Moyer, 1976.)

THE LIMITATIONS OF
PHYSIOLOGICAL CONTROL

The control techniques discussed above are powerful, but their limitations should be clearly understood. These methods would be ineffective in controlling the aggressive actions of a "trigger man" for Murder Incorporated, or those of a bomber pilot over North Vietnam. Both are engaged in instrumental aggression, and neither may have any feeling of hostility toward his victims. When his radar indicates that it is time to press his bomb release button, the pilot may do so without the slightest feeling of antagonism. His bombs may destroy the homes and lives of hundreds of people. He has behaved as he has been trained to behave and emotional responses may not be involved at all. The "trigger man" kills for financial reward; he may not know his victim and may feel no animosity toward him whatsoever.

These individuals have engaged in learned behavior. As of now, there is no physiological manipulation that can selectively effect learned responses. Further, with the current state of the art, no such method is likely to be found in the near future—and it is not even clear where to start looking. That kind of control must await major, and as yet quite unpredictable, breakthroughs.

The distinction between instrumental aggression and aggressive aggression containing an affective component has important implications for the abuse potential of the physiological control of aggression. The use of physiological controls may, in fact, be counterproductive for an individual who wishes to control the rebellious tendencies of a particular population. One reaction to oppression, political or otherwise, is to become angry and as a result of that anger, to evolve a plan, which may involve aggressive behavior, to alleviate the oppression. Another reaction to oppression is to recognize it as such intellectually and to come to the conclusion that the oppression must be eliminated. A plan, which may involve aggressive behavior, is then worked out. Antihostility drugs in the water supply or other physiological measures will affect only the anger, they will have no influence on the intellectual processes involved in the aggressive plans. In fact, if the anger is controlled, the plans may be more effective because they will not involve the impulsive quality that often results from the urgency of anger. Further, because the emotional component will not function as a distractor, the intellectual processes may function more efficiently.

In 1971 Kenneth B. Clark started a monumental controversy when he suggested that the necessary resources
in the form of scientific personnel and research facilities
be mobilized "to reduce human anxieties, tension, hostili-
ties, violence, cruelty, and destructive power irrationalities
of man which are the basis of wars" (p. 1055). He further
suggested that world leaders accept and use the first form
of psychotechnological biochemical intervention that would
reduce or block the possibility they would use their power
destructively. He implied that the adequate use of the new
physiological technology of hostility control could eliminate
destructive wars. Since, as this paper has shown, a great
deal is now known about hostility control (and the potential
for further developments in those types of controls is great),
it is important to attempt to relate these developments to
Clark's proposals.

If one assumes that modern wars result from the impulsive behavior of world leaders who are acting in anger,
Clark's proposal would be a reasonable and adequate
antiaggression therapy for world leaders. It would, in fact,
significantly reduce the possibilities of armed conflict.
Further, given the current status of our understanding,
it is highly likely that a concentrated research program
could develop pharmaceutical agents that, either singly
or in combination, could eliminate feelings of anger and
hostility and the irrational decisions based on those feelings. A number of drugs are available now, but considerable research is needed to establish the types of aggressive behavior affected, and more needs to be known about
possible side effects. When these drugs are perfected, as
they certainly will be, and we know with some assurance
that there are minimal risks of such effects as paradoxical
reactions, I agree with Kenneth Clark that they should be
taken by those who hold positions of political power. If we
can believe the news reports, it would be well for Idi Amin
to start taking some of the pharmaceutical agents we have
available now. The world can ill afford the luxury of world

leaders who are subject to fits of anger that may result in impulsive and irrationally aggressive behavior.

However, the unfortunate fact is that although the psychotechnical revolution may ultimately reduce feelings of anger and their resultant behavior, it is not likely to eliminate war. Much, if not most, of the aggression involved in war is instrumental. That is, it is directed at achieving certain gains—the acquisition of territory, the settlement of disputed boundaries, the expansion of a sphere of influence, or the economic exploitation of another country. These motives may have essentially no emotional component and anger may play no role. Once again, it should be emphasized that no known physiological manipulation can selectively influence particular learned behaviors. The psychotechnological revolution is not even close to being able to influence those kinds of behavior; thus war based primarily on nonemotional motivations will not be curtailed by physiological manipulations.

SOME FINAL IMPLICATIONS

It can be seen from the preceding discussion that an understanding of the physiology of aggressive behavior provides some new insights into the complex problem of aggression and introduces a somewhat different view of man. The view reintroduces the importance of physiological mechanisms as contributors to the determination of behavior. Learning and environmental conditions influence behavior powerfully, but they clearly operate on a soma that may enhance or reduce their effects. There are wide individual differences in physiology among men. These differences are at times powerful determinants of behavior.

Man has always recognized that behavior can be changed by altering an individual's environment or experience. It must now be recognized that behavior can be changed, sometimes drastically, by altering the internal milieu. That conclusion is now inescapable. The implications of this view are profound, and will change history. Our understanding of the psychological mechanisms underlying behavior is in its infancy. However, as knowledge increases, powerful new forces for influencing our destiny will be available. The increase in our knowledge of atomic forces moved us into a new era. The increase in our understanding of the physiology of behavior will move us into another, and the effects will be even more profound.

REFERENCES

BANDLER, R. J. and K. E. MOYER (1970) "Animals spontaneously attacked by rats." Communications in Behavioral Biology 5, 177-182.

BEEMAN, E. A. (1947) "The effect of male hormone on aggressive behavior in mice." Physiological Zoology 20, 373-405.

BERNSTEIN, H. and K. E. MOYER (1970) "Aggressive behavior in the rat: Effect of isolation and olfactory bulb lesions." Brain Research, 75-84.

BLUMER, D. and C. MIGEON (1973) "Treatment of impulsive behavior disorders in males with medroxy-progesterone acetate." Presented at the annual meeting of the American Psychiatric Association, May.

BOLTON, R. (1973) "Aggression and hypoglycemia among the Qolla: A study in psychobiological anthropology." Ethnology 12, 227-257.

BREMER, J. (1959) Asexualization. New York: Macmillan.

BROOM, L. and P. SELZNICK, (1957) Sociology: A Text With Adapted Readings. New York: Harper & Row.

CAMPBELL, M. B. (1970) "Allergy and behavior: Neurologic and psychic syndromes," pp. 28-46 in F. Speer (ed.) Allergy of the Nervous System. Springfield, IL: Thomas.

CHATZ, T. L. (1972) "Management of male adolescent sex offenders." International J. of Offender Therapy 2, 109-115.

CLARK, K. B. (1971) "The pathos of power: A psychological perspective." American Psychologist 26, 1047-1057.

CROOK, W. G., W. W. HARRISON, S. E. CRAWFORD, and B. S. EMERSON (1961) "Systemic manifestations due to allergy: Report of fifty patients and a review of the literature on the subject." Pediatrics 27, 790-799.

DALTON, K. (1964) The Premenstrual Syndrome. Springfield, IL: Thomas.

——— (1961) "Menstruation and crime." British Medical J. 3, 1752-1753.

——— (1960) "Schoolgirls' misbehavior and menstruation." British Medical J. 2, 1647-1649.

——— (1959) "Menstruation and acute psychiatric illness." British Medical J. 1, 148-149.

DELGADO, J. M. R., V. MARK, W. SWEET, F. ERVIN, G. WEISS, G. BACH-Y-RITA, and R. HAGIWARA (1968) "Intracerebral radio stimulation and recording in completely free patients." Journal of Nervous and Medical Diseases, 147, 329-340.

——— (1963) "Cerebral heterostimulation in a monkey colony." Science 141, 161-163.

EGGER, M. D. and J. P. FLYNN (1963) "Effect of electrical stimulation of the amygdala on hypothalamically elicited attack behavior in cats." Journal of Neurophysiology 26, 705-720.

EISENBERG, B. C. (1970) "Etiology: inhalants," pp. 143-197 in F. Speer (ed.) Allergy of the Nervous System. Springfield, IL: Thomas.

FALCONER, M. A., D. HILL, A. MEYER, and J. L. WILSON (1958) "Clinical, radiological, and EEG correlations with pathological changes in temporal lobe epilepsy and their significance in surgical treatment," pp. 396-410 in M. Baldwin and P. Bailey (eds.) Temporal Lope Epilepsy. Springfield, IL: Thomas.

FREDERICHS, C. and H. GOODMAN (1969) Low Blood Sugar and You. New York: Constellation International.

GASTAUT, H. (1954) "Interpretation of the symptoms of 'psychomotor' epilepsy in relation to physiologic data on rhinencephalic function." Epilepsia 3, 84-88.

GLASER, G. H., R. J. NEUMAN, and R. SCHAFER (1963) "Interictal psychosis in psychomotortemporal lobe epilepsy: An EEG psychological study," pp. 345-365 in G. H. Glaser (ed.) EEG and Behavior. New York: Basic Books.

GODDARD, G. V. (1972) "Long term alteration following amygdaloid stimulation," pp. 581-596 in B. Eleftheriou (ed.) The Neurobiology of the Amygdala. New York: Plenum.

GOTTLIEB, P. M. (1970a) "Neuroallergic reactions to drugs," pp. 134-142 in F. Speer (ed.) Allergy of the Nervous System. Springfield, IL: Thomas.

——— (1970b) "Allergic neuropathies and demyelinative disease," pp. 79-121 in F. Speer (ed.) Allergy of the Nervous System. Springfield, IL: Thomas.

HEATH, R. G. et al. (1954) Studies in Schizophrenia. Cambridge, MA: Harvard Univ. Press.

HEIMBURGER, R. F., C. C. WHITLOCK, and J. E. KALSBECK (1966) "Stereotaxic amygdalotomy for epilepsy with aggressive behavior." J. of the Amer. Medical Assoc. 198, 165-169.

KAHN, I. S. (1927) "Pollen toxemia in children." J. of the Amer. Medical Assoc. 88, 241-242.

KING, H. E. (1961) "Psychological effects of excitation in the limbic system," pp. 477-486 in D. E. Sheer (ed.) Electrical Stimulation of the Brain. Austin: University of Texas Press.

LAGERSPETZ, K. "Studies on the aggressive behavior of mice." Annales Academiae Scientiarum Fennicae Series B, 131, 1-131.

LYGHT, C. E. (1966) [ed.] The Merck Manual of Diagnosis and Therapy. West Point, PA: Merck.

MARK, V. H. and F. R. ERVIN (1970) Violence and the Brain. New York: Harper & Row.

MORTON, J. H., H. ADDITION, R. G. ADDISON, L. HUNT, and J. J. SULLIVAN (1953) "A clinical study of premenstrual tension." Amer. J. of Obstetrics and Gynecology 65, 1182-1191.

MOYER, K. E. (1976) The Psychobiology of Aggression. New York: Harper & Row.

——— (1968) "Kinds of aggression and their physiological basis." Communications in Behavioral Biology 2, 65-87.

NARABAYASHI, H., T. NAGAO, Y. SAITO, M. YOSHIDO, and M. NAGAHATA (1963) "Stereotaxic amygdalotomy for behavior disorders." Archives of Neurology 9, 1-16.

RANDOLPH, T. G. (1962) Human Ecology and Susceptibility to the Chemical Environment. Springfield, IL: Thomas.

ROBINSON, B. W., M. ALEXANDER, and G. BOWNE (1969) "Dominance reversal resulting from aggressive responses evoked by brain telestimulation." Physiology and Behavior 4, 749-752.

SANO, K. (1962) "Sedative neurosurgery: With special reference to posteromedial hypothalamotomy." Neurologia medico-chirurgica, 4, 112-142.

SCHAFFER, N. (1953) "Personality changes induced in children by the use of certain antihistaminic drugs." Annals of Allergy 11, 317-318.

SCHREINER, L. and A. KLING (1953) "Behavioral changes following rhinencephalic injury in cat." J. of Neurophysiology 16, 643-658.

SCHWAB, R. S., W. H. SWEET, V. H. MARK, R. N. KJELLBERG, and F. R. ERVIN (1965) "Treatment of intractable temporal lobe epilepsy by stereotactic amygdala lesions." Trans. of Amer. Neurological Assoc. 90, 12-19.

SEM-JACOBSEN, C. W. (1968) Depth-electrographic Stimulation of the Human Brain and Behavior. Springfield, IL: Thomas.

SERAFETINIDES, E. A. (1970) "Psychiatric aspects of temporal lobe epilepsy," pp. 155-169 in E. Niedmeyer (ed.) Epilepsy: Modern Problems in Pharmacopsychiatry. New York: Karger.

SPEER, F. (1970) "Etiology: foods," pp. 198-209 in F. Speer (ed.) Allergy of the Nervous System. Springfield, IL: Thomas.

——— (1954) "The allergic tension-fatigue syndrome." Pediatric Clinic of North America 1, 1029-1037.

SWEET, W. H., F. ERVIN, and V. H. MARK (1969) "The relationship of violent behavior to focal cerebral disease," pp. 336-352 in S. Garattini and E. B. Sigg (eds.) Aggressive Behaviour. New York: John Wiley.

WALKER, A. E. and D. BLUMER (1972) "Long term effects of temporal lobe lesions on sexual behavior and aggressivity." Presented at the Houston Neurological Symposium on Neural Bases of Violence and Aggression, Houston, Texas: March 9-11.

WHEATLEY, M. D. (1944) "The hypothalamus and affective behavior in cats." Archives of Neurology and Psychiatry 52, 296-316.

WOODS, J. W. (1956) "'Taming' of the wild Norway rat by rhinencephalic lesions." Nature 178, 869.

Benson E. Ginsburg
University of Connecticut

3

THE VIOLENT BRAIN
Is It Everyone's Brain?

While it is undoubtedly true that the proper study of mankind is man, it is also true that the human is the one organism we are least able to predict and control. There is one unique way in which we can know the human, and that is the sense in which each man is every man—the sense in which we share our common humanity. We can tell each other what we feel and why we acted as we did in a particular situation. We can observe and describe the actions of others. We even have sciences for doing this. We can also introspect, and through this introspection come to know our own feelings and to generalize these to other members of our species when they are in the same situation or experiencing similar moods.

One of the most terrifying of these moods is that of destructive, violent, rage, whether it is externalized or internalized, whether it is directed against others, or against one's self. To label it "maniacal" or to categorize it in other descriptive terms does not help us to understand it. To have given physical vent to such an emotion brings the participant very little closer either to self understanding or to the understanding of others who may act or have acted in the

AUTHOR'S NOTE: This research was supported by grant RR 00602 from the Animal Resources Branch of NIH and by grants from The Grant Foundation, Inc. and the Connecticut Research Foundation.

same way. We are all capable of killing, as witness what happens during time of war. Neither sex has a monopoly. Men and women commit suicide, murder, and participate in acts of violence and destruction, both as individuals and as members of groups. There are virtually no acts of savagery that can be imagined that have not been perpetrated: Torture, burning at the stake, whipping, maiming, lynching, drawing and quartering, have all received institutionalized sanction. Direct contact with the victim and the witnessing of his or her degradation, suffering, and death throes do not necessarily serve as deterrents (Lorenz, 1963). Public hangings, floggings, mutilations occur in parts of the world today. The savagery perpetrated against Armenians, Jews, Blacks, political dissidents, and other minorities within our own generation occurred among people like ourselves who were members of "cultured" and "civilized" communities. Lynching parties, including man-hunts that had all the earmarks of the so-called "sport" of hunting animals, with the exception that the denouement was often grizzlier and far more hideous, occurred very recently in our society. The wanton, thrill-seeking violence, often with a sexual motive, depicted in *A Clockwork Orange* has its many counterparts in reality. Reading this piece of fiction or watching it on film does not lead to a sense of suspended disbelief. The recent depiction in book and film of the Manson murders (*Helter Skelter*) provides the real life analogue. Most of us participate vicariously, through the depiction of these acts, which form such prominent themes in our cultural media. They also excite imitation. Who can say what it would take to turn any one of us from observer to participant under the proper circumstances? In our own recent history, we have seen upper middle class youth, some highly educated, participating in acts of terror and violence because they purported to be acting against a corrupt establishment.

The list of examples could be expanded and every one of you could provide your own. When has a person engaging in violence crossed the line from normal psychological and physiological functions to clinically aberrant behavior that is grounded in pathology? Perhaps the criterion is whether this is characteristic and driven behavior, or whether it is rare and elicited under the influence of drugs, social pressure, threat, or other circumstances that impel powerfully toward such behavior, as in the case of real or imagined self-defense, revenge, retaliation—or as an orgiastically sanctioned social, political or societal event, whether the sanctions are religious (saving the souls of the infidels), political (revolution, terror), or war. If there is a special pathology needed to participate in sadistic acts of cruelty, then, like the common cold, it can potentially infect any or all of us.

Attempts to analyze such truly frightening phenomena have resulted in a number of generalizations. One of these is the we-they dichotomy. To inflict direct torture and physical abuse on others, it is necessary to either justify it or to dehumanize the victims. "They" are pigs, niggers, Jews, heathens, Japs, Krauts, rapists, oppressors, degenerates, criminals, but they are not like us. At the same time, and perhaps at another level of realization, we know very well that they *are* like us, and that they are even, perhaps, the wrong victims—but, no matter, they will serve as warnings to others.

It is not only tempting to refer the seat and motive of these behaviors to the so-called lower centers that have escaped from rational control; but this is one prevailing mode of analysis. Another is to refer to evolution gone wrong, as Lorenz (1963) has done in his book, *On Aggression.* To simplify somewhat, but not overly, the notion is that the mechanism of the appeasement gesture that would turn off the attack in nonhuman encounters involving violence, either cannot be made (as in shooting or bombing from a distance), or the appropriate biological response that should turn off the aggressive behavior is not forthcoming. Lorenz's answer to these evolutionary deficiencies appears to be to cultivate rationalizations and displacement behaviors, such as sports, which release passions.

We know, undeniably, that there are biological parameters involved in various aspects of aggressive behavior. Brain stimulation and lesion studies show that certain structures, when stimulated, give rise to manifestations of aggressive behavior (Bard, 1948, 1950; Ervin et al., 1969; Flynn, 1967; Hess, 1954; Hess and Akert, 1955). Among the more dramatic studies in this realm are those involving electrodes implanted in specific brain areas to both elicit and inhibit attacks through stimulation of these areas in various social contexts, as, for example, in monkeys living in organized social groups and at various levels in the dominance hierarchy (Delgado, 1966, 1967a, and 1967b). As a matter of fact, these techniques would enable one to stop a charging bull with appropriate stimulation.

These methods have also been used clinically as part of a patient actuated feed-back system in which, by means of radio transmission, implanted electrodes, and computer analyses, it is possible to detect a changing mood using EEG patterns, and to send a signal to an implanted electrode in another part of the brain to alter the mood and the aggressive consequences that would otherwise follow (Delgado, 1969a and 1969b).

There is, demonstrably, a physical, anatomical, and physiological substratum for aggressive behavior and there are means for analyzing it and controlling it. We cannot, however, create a nation of persons implanted with electrodes feeding into computers that can program their reactions, nor would we wish to. Less drastic techniques, including behavior modification, psychotherapy, and chemotherapy have also been proposed and tried, as has psychosurgery, for which the moral as well as the scientific dilemmas were so well epitomized in *One Flew Over the Cuckoo's Nest*.

If education, displacement activities (such as sports), and other benign approaches are not efficacious, and if more drastic methods of attempted control, such as the ones cited, are abhorrent, impractical, and subject to easy abuse, what is the alternative? Do we simply ban violence and reports of violence in the public media, extol and reward other aspects of human behavior, and remove the perpetrators of violent acts from our society in the hope that this will diminish such behaviors, provide other outlets, and, in time, change behavioral norms? Or is this doomed to failure because of the structure and fabric of society itself, and because it is counter to our inner nature? What, in fact, is the nature of our biological nature, and what do we know scientifically about the biology of aggression?

Given that we are conditioned by our surroundings and respond to our circumstances, these interact with an underlying biological substratum which is presumably involved in aggression. We see this in one form or another in our mammalian and vertebrate ancestors, where dominance hierarchies were formed and related to the organization of social groups (DeVore, 1965; Jay, 1968; Johnson, 1972; Rabb et al., 1967; Scott, 1958). In addition to hunting and killing prey, there are ingroup-outgroup relationships within the same species, including monkey and baboon troops, wolf packs, and so forth. I have hypothesized elsewhere that the major evolutionary function of this behavior is to promote more rapid genetic diversification, and, therefore, enhance the possibility of adaptive change within a species (Ginsburg, 1968). This is because the genetic mechanism is essentially conservative, and were random mating to occur within a species, even given the usual forces of selection and mutation, the tendency would be toward an equilibrium of distribution of genotypes and phenotypes. Breaking up the population into small interbreeding groups promotes different genetic combinations in different parts of the population, such that the selective processes are speeded up and magnified. Aggressive behavior, therefore, comes into play and has been adaptive at several levels: that of hunting, that of protecting territory, that of maintaining the identity and cohesiveness of a group within its species, and that of organizing the relationships among members of a group.

Viewed in this way, the situation poses an intellectual dilemma. It would seem that the more aggressive individuals would be favored by processes of genetic selection, and assuming a genetic basis for such behavior, species would become more and more aggressive. One could speculate that this might reach a point where it would become disruptive, and therefore be selected against, or that selection operates in a different manner.

Some of the studies that we have done with wolf packs indicate that the latter is true (Rabb et al., 1967). Group organization is maintained through a complex system of communication and social roles in which serious fighting is an uncommon feature. Success in leaving progeny is not a direct or linear function of individual social dominance. It inheres in the group. The lack of correlation between individual social dominance and success in leaving progeny on the part of males has been observed among wolves, and has also recently been found for macaques (Ommen, 1975). The individuation of social roles among organized social mammals and the development of communications that avoid undue aggression, have most probably been achieved through group selection and are the pattern that the selective processes have taken.

All of this assumes that there are genetic differences in individual predisposition toward agonistic behavior that interact in a complex manner with environmental circumstances and involve neural mechanisms that have been associated with rage and attack behavior as indicated by the work of Bard, Delgado, Flynn, Hess and many others.

My own experience in this area has been documented elsewhere, but let me recapitulate it here as a series of stepping stones to the thesis that I wish to present.

Guinea pigs are not a highly social species and are not generally thought of as aggressive. As a graduate student working in the laboratory of Professor Sewell Wright on the genetics of coat color in guinea pigs, a number of us had the common experience of being consistently bitten by particular animals, though most of the others were quite benign in their behavior. Since this was a genetics laboratory, and the animals were reared and treated alike, we checked the pedigrees of the troublesome animals. They traced to Professor Wright's so-called family "A" and seldom if ever occurred in other genealogical lines within the colony. Family "A" was eventually eliminated because of its behavioral characteristics, representing a laboratory selection experiment against one form of aggressive behavior, and this solved the problem while, at the same time, providing evidence that it had a genetic basis (Ginsburg, 1971).

A similar situation occurred in the rabbit colony of Dr. Paul Sawin, where, in particular families of rabbits, regardless of the conditions of rearing, animals of both sexes were prone to attack, bite, kick, and scratch the caretakers and other personnel. We obtained some of these rabbits and bred them selectively. One of my former graduate students, Dr. Jerome Woolpy, now at Earlham College, devised a series of tests for the aggressive behavior, and it was again demonstrated that this had a genetic basis (Ginsburg, 1971).

To add a second dimension to this problem—that of genotype-environmental interaction—the work of Dr. A. Fisher using dogs, as well as some of our own observations using dingoes, provide illustrations of the diversity of these interactions (Fisher, 1955). Fisher was working with pedigrees of aggressive terriers at The Jackson Laboratory. They normally showed intense agonistic behavior when kept as litters which were reared together. If one isolated the littermates from an early age and fed them by hand, then placed them together after the normal weaning period, they could be reared together without the displays of unusual aggression that would otherwise occur. Cross-fostering terriers onto beagle mothers or vice versa did not change the characteristics of the behavior typical of these particular genealogies within these breeds. The beagles were not, for example, made aggressive if reared with terriers on terrier mothers. Hand-reared dingoes, on the other hand, maintained their aggressive behavior under analogous conditions where the terriers did not. As these examples illustrate, the behavior must have a genetic substratum, but this may differ so that its degree of lability under various conditions of rearing at critical times during the developmental history of the individuals will be distinctive for various genotypes.

This was further illustrated, dramatically, in mice. Dr. J. P. Scott, working at The Jackson Laboratory with three highly inbred mouse strains, each essentially representing a series of genetic replicates, found consistent fighting behavior among mature males tested after isolation in round-robin encounters within each strain and significant differences between them (Scott, 1942). When tested against each other, the C57BL/10 strain was clearly the least aggressive as judged in this paradigm. The late Dr. W. C. Allee was studying the same situation at the same time. As his research assistant, it was my task to carry out the experiments—as it happened—without knowledge that they were also being done elsewhere. My results were the opposite of Scott's, in that his most pacific strain was my most aggressive strain (Ginsburg and Allee, 1942). Allee then invited Scott to his laboratory, where he repeated his experiments using our mice and obtained his results. My attempts to replicate my results were also successful. There appeared to be no essential differences in our testing methods. However, the methods of handling the animals during the late pre-weaning period and into maturity were different. Scott weighed and transferred them by picking them up with a forceps by the tail; I handled them only minimally by scooping them up in a small box in which they were weighed, and tranferred them to the test cage by juxtaposing the entrances of the two cages and permitting the animal to move from one cage to the other by itself. Later investigations were carried out to determine whether any aspects of these handling differences applied at some stages of the life history of the mice could have accounted for the differences in the later results. As it turned out, these behavior differences did result from differences in handling for the C57BL/10 strain. However, the other two strains used in the investigation did not respond with the same lability (Ginsburg, 1967).

In a later investigation I was able to demonstrate, using a larger number of strains, that the optimal time for environmental input with respect to producing variation in agonistic behavior in males after sexual maturity, was strain-specific (Ginsburg, 1968b). Moreover, with the same handling procedures applied during the period of greatest sensitivity, some strains increased in aggressiveness while others decreased, and still others were unaffected by the procedures. These studies were extended by Dr. J. Jumonville who obtained comparable results with a larger diversity of genotypes (Jumonville, 1968).

As it turned out, our most aggressive strains were also susceptible to sound induced seizures. We had identified two autosomal genetic loci involved in the seizure mechanism (Ginsburg and Miller, 1963). There was a significant correlation between the seizure susceptibility and the tendency to high agrression among males that was associated with these loci and with tryptophan hydroxylase activity in strain comparisons and in segregation experiments, suggesting that the mechanisms involved in the seizures might also be involved in the tendency toward aggressive behavior. There is still another interconnection between these two behaviors, as shown in Table I. It is that animals exposed to a single seizure at weaning do not develop the expected aggressive behavior after sexual maturity (Ginsburg, 1968b).

While it is not yet clear how these changes come about, there are at least three neurochemical mechanisms known to be involved in the seizures: Schlesinger and co-workers have demonstrated that there is a correlation with the serotonergic mechanism and that the pharmacological manipulation of this mechanism results in a change in seizure susceptibility (Schlesinger et al., 1965). Dr. J. Diez, working in our laboratory, demonstrated an association between tryptophan hydroxylase, the rate-limiting enzyme for serotonin, and both seizures and aggression (Diez, 1973). Dr. J. Cowen, also working in our laboratory, demonstrated that one of the autosomal loci that my colleague Dr. Dorothea Miller and I had identified as involved in the seizures (and now presumably also in aggression) affects the activity of nucleoside triphosphatase (NTPase) in the granule cell layer of the dentate fascia (Cowen, 1966 and 1975; Ginsburg, 1967). The other locus is associated with glutamate metabolism and affects an inhibitory neural transmitter system, the glutamic acid decarboxylase-gamma aminobutyric acid (GAD-GABA) system (Cowen, 1966; Ginsburg et al., 1969; Sze, 1969). Dr. P. Y. Sze, in our laboratory, has demonstrated that the manipulation of this system during a particular phase of pre-weaning development can temporarily switch the underlying biochemical system from one level of activity to another and can thereby produce the counterpart of a genetically susceptible or genetically resistant animal (Sze, 1970). It has also been shown that this same system is affected by environmental input (sound priming) at these same stages of development and via the same mechanism. It is, therefore, our concept with respect to the genotype-environmental interaction that the mouse strains we are working with have the genetic capacity to produce GABA through glutamic acid decarboxylase activity at two different levels, one of which is associated with seizure susceptibility and also with aggressive behavior, and the other of which is not. We have identified mutants which essentially reprogram the individual during development so that it moves from one level of GAD activity to another. These mutants are associated with increasing the susceptibility to seizures of an otherwise resistant strain, and decreasing the susceptibility to seizures of an otherwise susceptible strain. Our concept, based on these and similar data, is that most individuals within the normal range of a population are genetically programmed for versatility. In this instance, they have the genetic capability to produce either level of GAD activity. This can be reprogrammed during development by introducing mutants whose effect is to favor one or another of these encoded genetic capabilities and therefore to regulate the system. The period at which the system is susceptible to genetic reprogramming also is the period during which environmental intervention, either pharmacologically or through appropriate stimulation, can favor one or another aspect of the genotype. We have referred to this concept as the "genomic repertoire" in contrast to the so-called "reaction range" that has been used to represent genotype environmental interactions (Dobzhansky, 1969; Ginsburg and Laughlin, 1971; Gottesman, 1974). The reaction range represents the concept that a given genotype will develop differently in various environmental conditions. If, therefore, one could observe it across the normative range of environments, one could characterize the reaction range. The concept of the genomic repertoire makes a further distinction—that of the difference between the encoded genotype and the effective genotype. It takes account of the fact that the encoded genotype contains many alternatives that are not used but may become available for use either in the presence of particular genes that interface with environmental events to regulate these systems, or they may be regulated more directly by environmental intervention. This makes it possible to research the mechanisms from a different point of view and to affect the outcome by reprogramming the potential already inherent in the individual. Obviously, this has very broad behavioral implications.

In pursuing these studies on agonistic behavior among male mice with Dr. J. Jumonville we found a number of strain-dependent effects of changing the intrauterine or neonatal environment (Jumonville, 1968). On closer inspection of the data derived from reciprocal crosses between high and low aggression strains, there appeared to be an association between the source of the Y-chromosome and the aggression score. Thus, in addition to two autosomal factors (which have now also been reported by others), there are also maternal factors and a Y-chromosome involvement.

The Y or male determining chromosome has been a controversial topic in aggression studies in humans. There is literature suggesting that individuals containing an extra Y-chromosome have certain characteristics in common, including tallness and a tendency toward aggressive behavior, and that they are found significantly above their expected proportions in prison populations representing individuals who have committed crimes of violence (Court-Brown, 1967; Daly, 1969; Price and Whatmore, 1967). The original studies have been critiqued on the basis of their sampling methods and evidence adduced that there is no invariable association between the extra Y and these aggressive tendencies (Hook, 1973; Shah, 1970). In humans, another interesting question intrudes itself, and that is the degree to which the behavior is driven by the biological situation, on the assumption that at least some XYY males have an unusual tendency toward aggression. Assuming this to be the case in these instances, the possibility exists that these impulses can be modified and controlled through appropriate patterns of rearing and training. As is now well publicized, this problem has also been criticized from an ethical point of view. If there is insufficient evidence that XYY always, or even generally, predisposes to unusual aggression, then identifying XYY infants and following them as though they were at risk for aberrant behavior might involve a self-fulfilling prophecy. On the assumption that this relationship is worth knowing more about, the experiments are continuing, but various safeguards have been introduced to prevent stigmatizing such persons.

The animal studies suggesting that the source of the single Y-chromosome (the normal attribute of all males) has an effect on aggressive behavior, lends credence to the idea that some XYY individuals would be so predisposed while others would not, since different Y-chromosomes are not equivalent with respect to their effects on these behaviors, and since various autosomal genes are also involved.

In our own studies, we have now moved from the demonstration that the source of the Y-chromosome can be associated with the aggression score of male mice, to the investigation of the mechanism by means of which these differential effects may be brought about (Ginsburg, 1971; Ginsburg and Sze, 1975; Selmanoff, 1974).

In a variety of experiments, it has been demonstrated that there is an association between androgen levels and social dominance in barnyard fowl, as well as other vertebrates, including mammals, and that so far as mice are concerned, early castration leads to absence of fighting behavior, although later castration leads only to diminution (Barkley, 1974; Beeman, 1947). Hormone replacement by implanted testosterone pellets or administration of androgen through silastic implants restores and augments the aggressive behavior. It requires a lesser dose to do this in adult pubertal castrates than in adult neonatal castrates. Classically it has been thought that prenatal or neonatal androgen conditions the nervous system for male behavior that is expressed postpubertally. In a series of collaborative experiments with Drs. J. Weisz and J. Diez, we were unable to find such an early association between plasma testosterone levels, as measured by radioimmunoassy, and either the source of the Y-chromosome or later aggressive behavior. Dr. M. Barkley (1974), working in the laboratory of Dr. Bruce Goldman, demonstrated that male hormone could be administered at various times after early castration, and that such administration at relatively low doses would have an organizing or priming effect with respect to agonistic behavior of males if a second dose were administered and maintained some three weeks later. It, therefore, appeared reasonable to suppose that the differential effects of the Y-chromosome might depend on priming at puberty. This was investigated by Dr. M. Selmanoff (1974), working collaboratively with our laboratory, and that of Dr. Goldman, who found that there was, indeed, an association between one of our "aggressive Y's" and an augmented pubertal surge of male hormone (Selmanoff et al., 1975 and 1976). After full sexual maturity, when the mice were tested for aggression scores, there were no significant hormone differences. Likewise, in following the developmental testosterone curves every three days from birth, there were no developmental differences except during the pubertal surge. It is, therefore, reasonable to assume as a hypothesis that the period of early puberty is the time of lability from the point of view of the organizing effects of testosterone on the brain for behaviors that depend on the continued maintenance of normal testosterone levels at full sexual maturity. Since not all "high aggression Y-chromosomes" are associated with such a pubertal surge, there is evidently more than one way in which the Y-chromosome produces effects on this aspect of behavior, at least in the mouse. Augmenting the pubertal surge in normal mice can mimic this effect. Attempts to maintain the pubertal surge within normal limits, where it occurs in association with high aggression, are now being made.

If this is a valid model for the human, it should, in theory, be possible to identify high risk individuals at puberty and through temporary treatment at this critical phase of their development (possibly by means of anti-androgens), to prevent any abnormal neural priming from occurring.

There are other data to suggest that these systems that we are researching in the mouse have implications for our own species. Dr. D. Lewis and co-workers (forthcoming, a, b) have been studying juveniles remanded to the court for violent behaviors. There are familial trends within their samples, and some findings suggestive of a relationship to some of the mechanisms and conditions associated with genetic predisposition to high aggressive behavior in the mouse. There are, for example, hallucinatory auras and psychomotor seizures in some of these children, but no overt clonic-tonic seizures. Although these data will have to be carefully evaluated and further confirming instances obtained if the analogy is to become meaningful, it is at least suggestive. Whether, if the analogy is maintained, there is also a homology of mechanism will remain to be established. On the assumption that some such instances will be found, we will have improved both our diagnostic and our therapeutic procedures with respect to biological predispositions for violent behavior. Such predispositions would, on the bases of these analogies, be expected to occur for a variety of different biological reasons, as well as through neurological damage and unusual life experiences. Even familial tendencies may be referred to the latter conditions. The possibility remains, however, that some stigmata will be characterizable as genetic risks in particular genealogies and that these will differ from one genealogy to another. Some of these risks may well involve the mechanisms found in other mammals, including the mouse. If this is true, it should be possible to identify the basis for each syndrome and to alleviate it by appropriate pharmacological or behavioral intervention at the appropriate time during development. Following these leads in the mouse research, it should be possible to reprogram the individual's existing genomic repertoire. There is nothing here suggestive of the hazards of more extreme procedures, such as psychosurgery, castration, or even treatment with psychoactive drugs that must be maintained and that may dull perception and interfere with other aspects of behavior. We do not know to what extent these biological mechanisms may drive and control the human, such that violent episodes become a highly probable mode of reaction. We will only find out by means of further research, which, at least, promises to provide the means for diagnosis and intervention that will essentially identify particular abnormal mechanisms and provide the tools for restoring them to normality by means of genetic reprogramming.

REFERENCES

BARD, P. and V. B. MOUNTCASTLE (1948) "Some forebrain mechanisms involved in the expression of rage with special reference to suppression of angry behavior." Proc. Assn. Res. Nerv. Ment. Disease 27: 362-404.

BARD, P. (1950) "Central nervous mechanisms for the expression of anger in animals," in M. L. Reymert (ed.) Feelings and Emotions. New York: McGraw-Hill.

BARKLEY, M. S. (1974) "Testosterone and the ontogeny of sexually dimorphic aggression in the mouse." Ph.D. dissertation, University of Connecticut.

BEEMAN, E. A. (1947) "The effect of male hormone on aggressive behavior in mice." Physiol. Zool. 20: 373-405.

BUGLIOUSI, V. and C. GENTRY (1974) Helter Skelter. New York: Norton.

BURGESS, A. (1962) A Clockwork Orange. London: Heinemann.

COURT-BROWN, W. M. (1967) Human Population Cytogenetics. New York: John Wiley.

COWEN, J. S. (1975) A genetic analysis of hippocampal variation associated with audiogenic seizures in the mouse." Ph.D. dissertation, University of Connecticut.

——— (1966) "A metabolic hippocampal anomaly associated with hereditary susceptibility to sound-induced seizures." M. S. thesis, University of Chicago.

DALY, R. F. (1969) "Mental illness and patterns of behavior in 10 XYY males." J. Nerv. Ment. Dis. 149: 318-327.

DELGADO, J.M.R. (1969a) Physical Control of the Mind. New York: Harper & Row.

——— (1969b) "Radio stimulation of the brain in primates and man." J. Int. Anesthetic Res. Soc. 48: 529-542.

——— (1967a) "Social rank and radio-stimulated aggressiveness in monkeys." J. Nerv. Ment. Dis. 144: 383-390.

——— (1967b) "Aggression and defense under central radio control." UCLA Forum in Medical Science 7: 171-193.

——— (1966) "Aggressive behavior evoked by radio stimulation in monkey colonies." Amer. Zool. 6: 669-681.

DEVORE, I. [ed.] (1965) Primate Behavior: Field Studies of Monkeys and Apes. New York: Holt, Rinehart & Winston.

DIEZ, J. A. (1973) "Genetic variation and the role of adrenal function in the regulation of serotonin and catecholamine synthesis in developing an adult mouse brain." Ph.D. dissertation, University of Connecticut.

DOBZHANSKY, Th. (1969) Genetics and the Origin of Species. New York: Columbia Univ. Press.

ERVIN, F. R., V. H. MARK and J. STEVENS (1969) "Behavioral and affective responses to brain stimulation in man," pp. 54-65 in J. Zubin and C. Shagass (eds.), Neurobiological Aspects of Psychopathology. New York: Grune & Stratton.

FISHER, A. E. (1955) "The effects of differential early treatment on the social and exploratory behavior of puppies." Ph.D. dissertation, Pennsylvania State University.

FLYNN, J. P. (1967) "The neural basis of aggression in cats." In D. C. Glass (ed.), Neurophysiology and Emotion. New York: Rockefeller Press and Russell Sage Foundation.

GINSBURG, B. E. (1971) "The role of genic activity in the determination of sensitive periods in the development of aggressive behavior," pp. 165-175 in J. Fawcett (ed.) Dynamics of Violence. Chicago: American Medical Association.

————(1968a) "Breeding structure and social behavior of mammals: a servomechanism for the avoidance of panmixia," pp. 117-128 in D. Glass (ed.) Genetics, Biology and Behavior. New York: Rockefeller Univ. Press and Russell Sage Foundation.

———— (1968b) "Genotypic factors in the ontogeny of behavior." Sci. and Psychoanalysis 12: 12-17.

———— (1967) "Genetic parameters in behavioral research," pp. 135-153 in J. Hirsch (ed.) Behavior-Genetic Analysis. New York: McGraw-Hill.

GINSBURG, B. E. and P. Y SZE (1975) "Pharmacogenetic studies of the serotonergic system in association with convulsive seizures in mice," pp. 85-95 in B. K. Bernard (ed.) Aminergic Hypotheses of Behavior: Reality or Cliche? Rockville, MD: National Institute on Drug Abuse.

GINSBURG, B. E. and W. S. LAUGHLIN (1971) "Race and intelligence, what do we really know?" pp. 77-82 in R. Cancro (ed.) Intelligence, Genetic and Environmental Influences. New York: Grune and Stratton.

GINSBURG, B. E. and D. S. MILLER (1963) "Genetic factors in audiogenic seizures," pp. 217-225 in R. G. Busnel (ed.) Psychophysiologie, Neuropharmacologie et Biochimie de la Crise Audiogene. Paris: Centre National de la Recherche Scientifique, No. 112.

GINSBURG, B. E. and W. C. ALLEE (1942) "Some effects of conditioning on social dominance and subordination in inbred strains of mice." Physiol. Zool. 15: 485-506.

GINSBURG, B. E., J. S. COWEN, S. C. MAXSON and P. Y. SZE (1969) "Neurochemical effects of gene mutations associated with audiogenic seizures," pp. 695-701 in A. Barbeau and J. R. Brunette (eds.) Progress in Neuro-Genetics. Amsterdam: Excerpta Medica.

GOTTESMAN, I. I. (1974) "Developmental genetics and ontogenetic psychology," pp. 55-80 in A. D. Dick (ed.) Minnesota Symposium on Child Psychology, Vol. 8. Minneapolis, MN: Univ. of Minnesota Press.

HESS, W. R. (1954) Diencephalon, Autonomic and Extrapyramidal Functions. New York: Grune and Stratton.

———— and K. AKERT (1955) "Experimental data on role of hypothalamus in mechanisms of emotional behavior." Arch. Neurol. Psychiat. 73: 127-129.

HOOK, E. B. (1973) "Behavioral implications of the human XYY genotype." Science 179: 139-150.

JAY, P. [ed.] (1968) Primates, Studies in Adaptation and Variability. New York: Holt, Rinehart and Winston.

JOHNSON, R. N. (1972) Aggression in Man and Animals. Philadelphia: W. B. Saunders.

JUMONVILLE, J. E. (1968) "Influence of genotype-treatment interactions in studies of 'emotionality' in mice." Ph.D. dissertation, University of Chicago.

KESEY, K. (1962) One Flew Over the Cuckoo's Nest. New York: Viking.

LEWIS, D. O. (in press, a) "Delinquency, psychomotor epileptic symptomatology and paranoid symptomatology: A triad." Amer. J. Psychiat.

LEWIS, D. O., D. BALLA, S. SHANAK, L. SNELL, and J. HENISZ (in press, b) "Delinquency, parental psychopathology and parental criminality: Clinical and epidemiological findings." J. Amer. Acad. Child Psychiat.

LORENZ, K. (1963) On Aggression. New York: Harcourt Brace & World.

OMMEN, G. (1975) Personal communication.

PRICE, W. H. and P. B. WHATMORE (1967) "Behavior disorders and patterns of crime among XYY males identified at a maximum security hospital." Brit. Med. J. 69: 533-536.

RABB, G. B., J. H. WOOLPY and B. E. GINSBURG (1967) "Social relationships in a group of captive wolves." Amer. Zool. 7: 305-311.

SCHLESINGER, K., W. BOGGAN and D. X. FREEDMAN (1965) "Genetics of audiogenic seizures. I. Relation to brain serotonin and norepinephrine in mice." Life Sci. 4: 2345-2351.

SCOTT, J. P. (1958) Aggression. Chicago: Univ. of Chicago Press.

——— (1942) "Genetic differences in the social behavior of inbred strains of mice." J. Hered. 33: 11-15.

SELMANOFF, M. K. (1974) "Genetic variation and the role of testosterone in the development and adult expression of aggression in inbred mice." Ph.D. dissertation, University of Connecticut.

——— S. C. MAXSON and B. E. GINSBURG (1976) "Chromosomal determinants of inermale aggressive behavior in inbred mice." Behav. Genet. 6: 53-69.

SELMANOFF, M. K., J. E. JUMONVILLE, S. C. MAXSON and B. E. GINSBURG (1975) "Evidence for a Y chromosomal contribution to an aggressive phenotype in inbred mice." Nature 253: 529-530.

SHAH, S. A. (1970) Report on the XYY Chromosomal Abnormality. National Institute of Mental Health conference report. Washington, DC: Government Printing Office.

SZE, P. Y. (1970) "Neurochemical factors in auditory stimulation and development of susceptibility to audiogenic seizures," pp. 259-269 in B. L. Welch and A. S. Welch (eds.) Physiological Effects of Noise. New York: Plenum.

——— (1969) "Neurochemical factors in the development of genetically determined susceptibility to audiogenic seizures in the mouse." Ph.D. dissertation, University of Chicago.

Patrick S. Dynes
Ohio State University
Eric W. Carlson
University of Arizona
Harry E. Allen
San Jose State University

4

AGGRESSIVE AND SIMPLE SOCIOPATHS
Ten Years Later

In the fall of 1977, the Program for the Study of Crime and Delinquency began a retrospective study of the criminal careers of sociopaths over a ten-year period.[1] Our study was designed to examine the careers of various types of sociopathic and nonsociopathic felons through their preinstitutional, institutional and postinstitutional phases (Allen et al., 1978).

Sociopathy has both social and biological correlates (Allen, Lindner, Goldman and Dinitz, 1969). The social correlates of sociopathy characterize sociopaths as individuals who are particularly troublesome in that they are:

chronically antisocial individuals who are always in trouble, profiting neither from experience nor punishment, and maintaining no real loyalties to any person, group or code. They are frequently callous and hedonistic, showing marked emotional immaturity, with lack of sense of responsibility,

AUTHORS' NOTE: Presented at the panel "Aggression and Violence: Biology or Society?" of the Annual Meeting of the American Society of Criminology, Dallas, Texas, November 8-11, 1978.

lack of judgement, and ability to rationalize their behavior
so that it appears warranted, reasonable and justified
[American Psychiatric Association, 1968: 38].

Cleckley (1964) has provided one of the most detailed
accounts of sociopathy and its many manifestations. He
considered the main features of the disorder to be: superficial charm and good intelligence; absence of delusions
and other signs of irrational thinking; absence of nervousness or neurotic manifestations; unreliability, untruthful-
ness and insincerity; lack of remorse or shame; antisocial
behavior without apparent compunction; poor judgement
and failure to learn from experience; pathologic egocen-
tricity and incapacity for love; general poverty of major
affective relations; specific loss of insight; unresponsive-
ness in general interpersonal relations; fantastic and unin-
viting behavior with drink and sometimes without; suicide
threats rarely carried out; trivial and poorly integrated sex
life and failure to follow any life pattern.

On the other hand, the biological correlates of sociopathy
picture sociopaths as having electroencephalographic patterns which reveal delayed maturation of some cortical
neural mechanism (Goldman, 1973). Sociopaths have slow
wave electroencephalography which is associated with
lymbic system dysfunctions (Kiloh and Osselton, 1966).
They have a decreased state of cortical excitability and
attenuated sensory input (Hare, 1970; Lindner et al., 1970).
Their aggressivity increases when treated with barbituates,
neuroleptics, and ethanol. Their need for stimulation shows
them to be at the low end of the arousal continuum (Quay,
1965). Stereotyped behavior, together with defective space-
time integration, suggests that sociopaths have basal gan-
glia dysfunctions (Dinitz et al., 1972; Dinitz et al., 1973).

Given the close ties of sociopathy and criminal behavior
presented in the literature, and the current focus of concern
on the chronically antisocial offender, an examination of
the impact of sociopathy on criminal careers seems war-

ranted (Dinitz, 1977; Dinitz and Conrad, 1978; Kittrie, 1971; Szasz, 1970). Few of the claims made about the impact of sociopathy on criminal careers have been based on empirical evidence. Two relevant empirical studies by Allen (1969) and Gatten (1973) have addressed this issue.

PREVIOUS STUDIES

Allen Study

The experimental group for the Allen (1969) study included 277 consecutive admissions (all male) to the maximum security Ohio Penitentiary. Classification procedures divided inmates into four categories: Hostile sociopaths, Simple sociopaths, Mixed subjects, and Nonsociopaths or Normals.[2] The study was unique in that it differentiated two major types of antisocial sociopaths. The Lykken Anxiety Scale (Lykken 1955, 1957) separated sociopaths into high Lykken sociopaths or "Hostile sociopaths" (Aggressive sociopaths), and low Lykken sociopaths or "Simple sociopaths."

Comparison of Hostile and Simple sociopaths on demographic characteristics, military and criminal histories, and psychological and attitudinal measures revealed marked differences between the two. A comparison of criminal history variables showed that Simple and Hostile sociopaths, considered either separately or as a group, performed consistently worse on almost all criminal justice variables. Criminal history variables also showed Simple sociopaths are a distinct group in that Simple sociopaths are likely to engage in more frequent but less aggressive antisocial behavior (Goldman et al., 1973). Simples, as compared with Hostile sociopaths, committed less than half the rate of crimes against the person, averaged more officially recorded arrests, more previous incarcerations, spent more of their adult lives behind bars, had four times the number of escapes, and showed more parole violations.

The Allen data make it clear that in addition to sociopaths being a typology distinct from Mixed and Nonsociopath offenders, the sociopath classification itself consists of a heterogeneous population. Previous attempts to treat them in a homogeneous fashion may account for the inability of previous research to isolate biogenetic, psychogenetic, and other significant differences between sociopathic inmate subjects (Dinitz et al., 1973).

Gatten Study

Gatten (1973) conducted a follow-up study of the same 277 inmates forty-two months after Allen in an attempt to determine if Simple and Hostile sociopaths had different institutional and postinstitutional adjustments. The results indicated that the study group classification—Simple, Normal, and so forth—was not as good a predictor of many institutional behaviors as was age and race. However, some differences did emerge. Simples spent less time in prison, yet were denied parole more often. Focusing on community adjustment, Gatten found that average arrests were as follows: .79 Nonsociopaths, .57 Simples, .49 Mixed, and .4 Hostiles. Simples were not arrested for alcohol offenses after release. Hostiles averaged more than twice as many parole violations as the other three groups.

RESEARCH DESIGN AND METHODOLOGY

The present study was designed to provide further evidence of long term social correlates of sociopathy in the criminal justice system. The sample for the present study is the same sample that Allen and Gatten used and this research completes the panel design and longitudinal study of the 277 consecutive admissions to the Ohio Penitentiary begun in 1967.

Since the Allen and Gatten studies had already collected data on social background variables, psychological test variables, and criminal justice variables, it was only necessary to collect follow-up criminal behavior data. This information was obtained from the files of the Ohio Adult Parole Authority. The following types of data were gathered:

parole number, escape attempts, parole date, final release date, number and type of arrests, number and type of incarcerations, drug or alcohol abuse, length of time to secure placement, length of time placed in the first year of parole, length of time on parole, parole violations, absconding, pre-release program participation, and participation in community based corrections.

Because of temporal and economic constraints, data on only 233 of the 276 consecutive admissions have been collected to date. The characteristics of this sample have been checked on social background variables, psychological test variables, and criminal justice variables, and no selection bias is evident (Kerlinger, 1973: 119).[3]

RESULTS

As a group, the parole outcomes encountered are not particularly unusual (Glaser, 1969; Waller, 1974) as shown in Table 4.1. More than nine out of ten inmates were released from prison during the ten year period (91.8%, N= 214). Of the 214 inmates paroled, approximately one in seven were reincarcerated following final release from their first parole and were then paroled for a second time (14%, N=30). Approximately one in fifty of the original parolees had a third parole (1.9%, N=4).

For the sake of brevity we will henceforth concentrate on the outcomes during the first parole. Of those making the first parole, more than a third received their parole during the first year of commitment (33.6%, N=72). By the

TABLE 4.1: Parole Outcomes for 233 Inmates

	%	N
Number of Paroles		
Never paroled	8.1	19
Paroled once	91.8	214
Parole twice	14.0	30
Paroled three times	1.9	4
Year of Parole		
1968	33.6	72
1969	19.2	41
1970	20.1	43
1971	9.8	21
1972	5.1	11
1973	4.7	10
1974	3.7	8
1975	2.3	5
1976	0.9	2
1977	0.5	1
Total		214
Final Release		
Got final release	75.5	160
No final release	24.5	52
Total		212
Year of Final Release		
1969	27.5	44
1970	18.1	29
1971	20.0	32
1972	13.7	22
1973	8.1	13
1974	7.5	12
1975	3.1	5
1976	1.9	3
1977	0.0	0
Total		160
Length of Time on First Parole		
Six months or less	5.2	11
Seven to twelve months	52.6	111
One to two years	31.3	66
Two to three years	5.2	11
Three to four years	4.7	10
More than four years	0.9	2
Total		211

TABLE 4.1: (Continued)

	%	N
Declared Parole Violator		
Declared parole violator at large	15.2	32
Not a parole violator	84.8	178
Total		210
Declared Parole Violator at Large		
Declared parole violator at large	15.6	33
Not a parole violator ar large	84.4	178
Total		211
Number of Times Arrested		
No arrests	55.2	116
One arrest	23.3	49
Two arrests	10.5	22
Three arrests	6.7	14
Four arrests	1.4	3
Five or more arrests	2.9	6
Total		210
Recommitted to an Institution		
Recommitted	23.2	49
Not recommitted	76.8	162
Total		211
Drug and/or Alcohol Abuse Problems		
No abuse	60.3	126
Alcohol abuse	32.1	67
Drug abuse	3.3	7
Both alcohol and drug abuse	4.3	9
Total		209
Prerelease Program		
No prerelease	95.0	209
Furloughed	4.1	9
Work-release	0.9	2
Total		209
Community Based Corrections		
No community based corrections	91.4	191
Halfway house	8.1	17
Community reintegration center	0.5	1
Total		209
Placement		
Not placed	36.3	74
Got job placement	57.4	117
Got educational placement	0.5	1
Got both job and educational placement	5.9	12
Total		204

end of the third year of incarceration, approximately three quarters of the parolees were released from prison (72.9%, N=156). Three quarters of the parolees received a final release from parole (75.5%, N=160) while one quarter were never finally released (24.5%, N=52). Of those receiving a final release (N=160), more than one quarter (27.5%, N=44) received it during 1969. More than six out of ten of those finally released were so released by the end of 1971 (65.6%, N=105). Almost six of ten spent a year or less on parole (57.8%, N=122). More than one in seven of the parolees were declared parole violators (15.2%, N=32), while approximately the same number of parolees absconded supervision (15.6%, N=33). More than four out of ten parolees were arrested at least once during their first parole (44.8%, N=94). More than one out of every five parolees were recommitted to an institution during their first parole (23.2%, N=49). Almost four out of ten parolees had drug or alcohol abuse problems while on parole (39.7%, N=83). Only one in twenty participated in a prerelease program (5%, N=11), while almost twice as many used community based corrections services (8.6%, N=18). More than a third were not placed at all during the first year of parole (36.3%, N=74).

Relationships Among Variables

One of our major objectives was to determine the relationship of the typology to the parole outcome variables. The types were Hostile, Mixed, Normal and Simple. The parole outcome variables were length of incarceration, the decision to parole, alcohol or drug abuse, arrests, parole violations, absconding, recommitments to an institution, and final release.

The results show that Simples took longer to be paroled.[4]

Mixed, Normal and Hostile types were all approximately equally likely to be paroled from prison, but Simples were more likely than all three types to be paroled.

Hostiles were the most likely to abuse alcohol or drugs, while the other three groups were equally abuse prone.

Hostiles were most likely to be arrested while on parole, Simples were next most likely to be arrested.

Simple sociopaths were most likely to be declared parole violators; Hostiles were the next most likely.*

Hostiles were the most likely to abscond from supervision; Simples were the least likely.*

Both Hostile and Simple sociopaths were more than twice as likely to be recommitted to an institution than were the other two groups.*

Almost twice as many Hostiles failed to obtain final release than any of the other three groups.

DISCUSSION AND SUMMARY

The aggregate performance of the experimental groups probably does not reveal any unexpected findings. On the other hand, when the group is subdivided into Hostile, Mixed, Normal and Simple, some important and significant findings emerge. First, contrary to Gatten's findings at forty-two months, Simple sociopaths took longer to be released from prison. Since Gatten has shown that their institutional behaviors were not much worse than the Mixed and Normal groups, it could be hypothesized that their more lengthy incarcerations and more frequent parole denials can most likely be attributed to the parole board basing its decision on their lengthy criminal records.

Second, both Simple and Hostile sociopaths were most likely to encounter difficulty while on parole. Both types of sociopaths were more likely to be arrested than Mixed or Normal types. Simples were most likely to be parole violators and Hostiles were most likely to be at large or abscond. This is consistent with Allen's earlier results that Simple sociopaths were most likely to be parole violators, as well as Gatton's claim that Hostile sociopaths are the most likely to be parole violators since neither distinguishes between a "parole violator" and a "parole violator at large." The sociopath's great propensity to violate parole is in line with the compulsive personality dimensions of the sociopath.

Third, and finally, both Simple and Hostile sociopaths were more than twice as likely to be recommitted to an institution. Allen showed that even ten years ago these sociopaths had a higher probability of being incarcerated.

Although these findings will not solve the dilemma of whether aggression and violence are biological or social phenomena, the results do offer evidence that typologies of persistently antisocial individuals can be constructed and implemented. The sociopath seems clearly to be a socially abnormal individual and his condition appears related to his criminal career. Whether his problems can be further linked to biological abnormalities must wait on the courts to again allow biological testing (Rennie, 1978; Sleffel, 1977). Certainly the development of effective management techniques to lessen the sociopath's disruptions will depend on the extent to which the problem is biological, social, or both.

NOTES

1. We would like to thank William Gilbert, George Farmer, Mary York, and Steve Van Dine of the Adult Parole Authority of the Ohio Department of Rehabilitation and Corrections for giving us access to their records.

2. The criteria used in the classification of these 277 consecutive admissions as Simple, Hostile, Mixed or Normal inmates includes: 1) the subjective ratings of the psychological services staff of each inmate on the sixteen item Cleckley Symptom Checklist; 2) the number of arrests since age eighteen; 3) the percentage of one's life incarcerated since age eighteen; 4) the MMPI scale 4 (Pd) minus scale 7 (Pt); 5) the presence of any recorded escapes from any penal or correctional setting such as jail, detention center, juvenile institution, or prison; and 6) the Lykken Activity Preference Questionnaire scale score.

3. The sample included 41 Hostiles, 21 Simples, 55 Mixed and 116 Nonsociopath subjects.

4. Here and elsewhere statistically (chi-square) significant relationships (.05) will be marked by an asterisk (*).

REFERENCES

ALLEN, H. E. (1969) "Bio-Social correlates of two types of anti-social sociopaths." Ph.D. Dissertation, Ohio State University.

———, E. W. CARLSON, and P. S. DYNES (1978) "Career life patterns: a cohort analysis of 274 criminal careers." Presented at the Twenty-Third Annual Southern Conference on Corrections, Tallahassee, Florida, March 6.

ALLEN, H. E., L. LINDNER, H. GOLDMAN, and S. DINITZ (1969) "The social and bio-medical correlates of sociopathy." Criminologica 6 (February).

——— (1971) "Hostile and simple sociopaths: an empirical typology." Criminology 9 (May): 27-47.

American Psychiatric Association (1968) The Diagnostic and Statistical Handbook of Mental Disorders. Washington, DC: American Psychiatric Association.

CLECKLEY, H. (1964) The Mask of Sanity. Saint Louis: Mosby.

DINITZ, S. (1977) "Chronically antisocial offenders," pp. 21-42 in John P. Conrad and Simon Dinitz (eds.) In Fear of Each Other. Lexington, MA: D. C. Heath.

——— and J. P. CONRAD (1978) "Thinking about dangerous offenders." Columbus, OH: Academy for Contemporary Problems.

DINITZ, S., H. GOLDMAN, H. E. ALLEN, and L. A. LINDNER (1973) "Psychopathy and autonomic responsivity: a note on the importance of diagnosis." J. of Abnormal Psychology 82, 3: 533-534.

DINITZ, S., H. E. ALLEN, H. GOLDMAN, and L. A. LINDNER (1972) "The juice model: a new look at sociopathy." et al., 3, 1: 20-28.

GATTEN, K., S. DINITZ, H. GOLDMAN, L. LINDNER, and H. E. ALLEN (1973) Pre-Institutional, Intramural and Parole Careers of Sociopaths: An Outcome Study. Columbus, OH: Program for the Study of Crime and Delinquency.

GOLDMAN, H. (1973) "Sociopathy and diseases of arousal." Quaderni di Criminologica Clinica 2: 113-125.

———, L. A. LINDNER, S. DINITZ, and H. E. ALLEN (1973) "The simple sociopath: physiologic and sociologic characteristics." Biological Psychiatry, 3: 77-83.

GLASER, D. (1969) The Effectiveness of a Prison and Parole System. Indianapolis: Bobbs-Merril.

HARE, R. D. (1970) Psychopathy: Theory and Research. New York: John Wiley.

KERLINGER, F. N. (1973) Foundations of Behavioral Research. New York: Holt, Rinehart and Winston.

KILOH, L. and J. W. OSSELTON (1966) Clinical Electroencephalography. Washington, DC: Butterworth.

KITTRIE, N. (1971) The Right To Be Different. Baltimore: Penguin.

LINDNER, L. A., H. GOLDMAN, S. DINITZ, and H. E. ALLEN (1970) "Antisocial personality type with cardiac liability." Archives of General Psychiatry 23 (September) 260-267.

LYKKEN, D. T. (1957) "A study of anxiety in the sociopathic personality." J. of Abnormal and Social Psychology, 55: 6-10.

——— (1955) "A study of anxiety in the sociopathic personality." Ph.D. Dissertation, University of Minnesota.

QUAY, H. (1965) "Psychopathic personaltiy and psychopathological stimulation seeking." Amer. J. of Psychiatry 122: 180-183.

RENNIE, Y. (1978) The Search for Criminal Man: A Conceptual History of the Dangerous Offender. Lexington, MA: D. C. Heath.

SLEFFEL, L. (1977) The Law and The Dangerous Criminal. Lexington, MA: D. C. Heath.

SZASZ, T. S. (1970) The Manufacture of Madness. New York: Dell.

WALLER, I. (1974) Men Released From Prison. Toronto, Canada: Univ. of Toronto Press.

Harold R. Holzman
U.S. Department of Justice

5

LEARNING DISABILITIES AND JUVENILE DELINQUENCY
Biological and Sociological Theories

INTRODUCTION

In the United States, Sociology has dominated the study of crime for some fifty years. Criminological textbooks have systematically underplayed the role of biological factors in the etiology of crime (Larson, 1977). Ironically, while adopting a "medical model" in its struggle to control crime, the criminological establishment in the United States has all but banished biological themes from the matrix of its discipline. It is not surprising then that most criminological theories that have evolved in the United States have not been informed by biological research into the causes of delinquency.

This paper will discuss the relationship of a specific set of biological phenomena—learning disabilities—to the genesis of juvenile delinquency. First, it will be shown that there is solid evidence that learning disabilities are a predisposing factor in the etiology of careers in delinquency. Second, it will be demonstrated that such evidence can plausibly be incorporated into existing sociological explanations of crime and thereby strengthen these explanations.

LEARNING DISABILITIES (LD)

Generally speaking, biological factors vis-a-vis the causes of behavior can be defined as those "processes and conditions that typically are considered as belonging to or characteristic of the organism" (Shah and Roth, 1974: 104). Learning disabilities can be broadly defined as impairments in sensory and motor functioning which lead to deviant classroom performance, and are the product of some abnormal physical condition (Valetutti, 1975).

Three major types of learning disabilities presently identified are dyslexia, aphasia, and hyperactivity. Dyslexia, first called word blindness, can be defined as "a disorder in children who, despite conventional classroom experience, fail to attain the language skills of reading, writing and spelling commensurate with their intellectual abilities" (Critchley, 1972: 11). Aphasia is generally characterized by problems in communicating verbally or problems in understanding the speech of others. An aphasic person may be able to understand written and spoken language but himself speak in disorganized sentences containing incorrect words (Pincus and Tucker, 1974: 113). Aphasia also may be characterized by the chronic inability to remember the names of everyday objects. Dyslexia has been characterized as a particular form of aphasia which involves one's understanding of and ability to manipulate written language (Murray et al., 1976: 13). Aphasia is usually associated with hearing and speech, while dyslexia primarily involves reading.

Hyperactivity (hyperkinesis) is "a long term childhood pattern characterized by excessive restlesness and inattentiveness" (Safer and Allen, 1976: 5). This persistent pattern of excessive activity in situations requiring motor inhibition (e.g., in the classroom), is chiefly characterized by an inability to maintain attention which in turn acts as an impediment to learning. Other features associated with hyperactivity are impulsivity, difficulty with peers (lack of popularity due to bothersome behavior), and low self-esteem (Safer and Allen, 1976: 9). Not unexpectedly, hyperactive children very often have behavior problems both at school and at home.

The causes of these three disorders are not well understood. There seems little argument, however, that they are biologically rooted. Hyperactivity has been associated with the mother's health during pregnancy, length of pregnancy, and condition of the child after delivery, e.g., respiratory distress (Safer and Allen, 1976: 11). Hyperactive children respond quite differently to stimulant medications than do "normal" youngsters. Also, children suffering from organic brain diseases exhibit symptoms similar to those of aphasics (Pincus and Tucker, 1974: 113). Furthermore, it is not unusual for electroencephalographic examinations of children exhibiting LD to yield abnormal patterns (Gross and Wilson, 1974). Despite evidence suggesting that LD is related to deviations of function in the central nervous system, the precise etiology of the disorders remains a mystery.

LEARNING DISABILITIES AND INAPPROPRIATE BEHAVIOR

Studies Comparing Delinquents and Non-Delinquents

It has long been recognized that juvenile delinquents tend to be poor students (President's Commission, 1967). Until recent years, however, little research has been done in comparing the incidence of LD among delinquents and nondelinquents. There are two studies comparing nondelinquents with delinquents in correctional facilities which do show LD to be more prevalent among delinquents. Hurwitz et al. (1972), found that delinquent boys had a higher incidence of sensory and motor problems than nondelinquent boys. Berman (1975) compared a group of delinquent boys with a group of delinquents of comparable age using the Halstead-Reitan battery of measures. He concluded that the groups differed significantly on those measures with delinquents displaying a greater frequency of symptoms associated with LD. It should be noted, however, that both these studies used N's of under fifty and dealt only with incarcerated delinquents.

Studies Comparing Children with LD
and Those Without LD

If one examines the research comparing the behavior patterns of "normal" children with those diagnosed as LD, one finds a great deal of evidence that supports the notion that the children with LD are much more apt to have behavior problems at school. The assertion is not being made here that all children who chronically misbehave at school become delinquents. It is, however, reasonable to assume that a child who is chronically in conflict with school authorities may reject school sufficiently to become involved in truancy or vandalism—if not more serious forms of delinquency. At a minimum, the child in constant conflict with his teachers will (1) probably not have very positive feelings about school; and (2) probably not be a good student. The two attributes are commonly found among delinquents (President's Commission, 1967).

Comparing two groups of 32 children ("normal" versus LD) chosen from the second and fifth grades, Gilbert (1976) found that LD students exhibited more behavior problems.

Grieger and Richards (1976) compared the classroom behavior of children with LD with "normal" children. One hundred LD children (18 girls, 82 boys) from elementary and intermediate special education classes and 527 youngsters from regular grades 1 through 7 composed the samples. The LD children were found to exhibit a higher incidence of problem conduct.

Ackerman et al. (1977), studied 3 groups of LD boys (23 hyperactives, 25 normoactives and 14 hypoactives) in grade school and reevaluated them at age 14. Half of the hyperactive boys were noted to have had major conflicts with authority.

A seven year longitudinal study of 500 children was conducted by Huessy and Cohen (1976) via teacher questionnaires in the second, fourth, fifth, and ninth grades. Teachers were asked about the presence of behavior problems with LD. The study's subjects represented all the second graders in several school districts. The 20% of the sample whose initial screening tests yielded the highest scores for LD accounted for 35% of those ninth graders with behavioral problems or academic maladjustment. Conversely, the 30% of the sample, who, as second graders, had the lowest scores for LD, displayed no discernible behavior or academic adjustment problems.

While those studies do not provide overwhelming evidence that LD and delinquency are definitely linked, they certainly support the notion that the possession of LD is a predisposing factor in the appearance of behavior problems in a classroom setting. While such an assertion concerning hyperactivity may seem eminently logical, it has been very slow in finding its way in criminological treatises on the possible causes of juvenile delinquency. The reader might ask himself if widely accepted theories of delinquency which focus on failure in the classroom in their explanation of delinquency are supported by quantitative research of the genre just presented.

THE POSSIBLE RELATIONSHIP BETWEEN LD AND JUVENILE DELINQUENCY

Some research suggests that there is a higher incidence of LD among the population of juvenile correctional facilities than there is among the nondelinquent population (Hurwitz et al., 1972, Berman, 1975). This research reinforces the notion held by some that learning disabilities are in general much more common among delinquents than nondelinquents. It should be emphasized however that evidence in support of that belief is presently very limited. Even if one were to establish through a series of large-scale screenings of adjudicated delinquents (both inside and outside of correctional facilities) and nondelinquents of comparable age, race, and social status that LD was more prevalent among delinquents, this alone would not prove that LD "caused" delinquency. It would only establish that the two were correlated. Delinquent behavior might have resulted in a child's development of symptoms or problems that are associated with LD.

To establish a link between LD and juvenile delinquency, it would have to be demonstrated that LD actually caused or at least predisposed children to engage in behavior likely to be defined as delinquent. It is the author's opinion that the existing research on the behavior of LD children in the school setting, part of which was presented in a preceding section of this paper, strongly suggests that the possession of a learning disorder, especially hyperactivity, inclines one toward behavior that is likely to be defined as inappropriate—if not actually delinquent. There is evidence to suggest that behavior problems of LD children are common early in elementary school, before most juveniles come into contact with the criminal justice system. Therefore, it might reasonably be concluded that temporally LD precedes misconduct and delinquency.

These behavioral difficulties may stem from several causes. In the case of untreated hyperactive children, poor impulse control might lead directly to inappropriate behavior and thus conflict with authority. Repeated disciplinary problems at school may lead a child to reject school completely. Thus he might embark on a career of truancy and delinquency, ultimately resulting in his becoming a client of the juvenile court. Nonhyperactive LD children may experience so much failure and frustration in school as to cause them to reject school and thus to engage in "acting out" behaviors clearly inappropriate to the academic environment. This chain of events might also ultimately result in truancy and delinquency with its attendent consequences. Finally, and perhaps a more subtle cause of misconduct, is the situation where the academic failure associated with LD is actually somewhat assuaged by placement in special education classes but where the child is not fully accepted by other children because of his disabilities, e.g., special student ("dummy") status, aggressive behavior, difficulties in communicating (Bruininks: 1978). Here, social failures may lead a child to reject the school environment or seek other, perhaps less suitable social arenas where he is both more successful and more socially acceptable, e.g., delinquent subcultures.

LEARNING DISABILITIES AND STRUCTURAL FUNCTIONALIST THEORIES OF DELINQUENCY

To varying degrees, Structural Functionalist explanations of juvenile delinquency like those of Cohen (1955), and Cloward and Ohlin (1961) have noted the failure of most clients of the juvenile justice system to succeed academically. The Structural Functionalist perspective involves the notion that the inability of the lower class child to succeed by conventional means (i.e., to meet the middle class standards of behavior and achievement that prevail in school) forces him to participate in delinquent subcultures where he can meet his status needs—albeit in unconventional ways. The reasons for the child's failure in school were seen by the Structural Functionalists as almost entirely sociological in nature.

The two basic criticisms of Structural Functionalist explanations of delinquency are: (1) the theory does not explain middle class delinquency; and (2) the theory assumes a core set of success values to which all members of the society are thought to subscribe. The recognition of LD as a possible predisposing factor in delinquency, however, provides an explanation of failure in the class-room and subsequent rejection of school, which is un-related to the issue of conflicting value systems that under-lies these two criticisms. Learning disabilities are found in children in all socioeconomic strata. Untreated hyper-activity can lead directly to socially unacceptable behavior in children who may not be troubled by their academic failures or the denial of access to legitimate opportunity structures. In essence, the presence of learning disabilities may cause children to reject school and perhaps pursue acceptance or success elsewhere. There may well be biological as well as sociological reasons for joining a delinquent subculture or rejecting legitimate opportunity structures in favor of illegitimate ones.

CONCLUSIONS

The possible link between learning disabilities and juvenile delinquency cannot be ignored. But there is no question that the evidence linking these two phenomena is limited and that more research is needed. Unfortunately, most of the current research on the relationship between learning disabilities and delinquency focuses on teenagers who have already been adjudicated delinquent. Existing research that touches on discipline problems of LD young-sters in elementary school suggests that the develop-ment of maladaptive behavior patterns starts very early in their educational careers. More longitudinal studies like that by Huessy and Cohen (1976) are needed to determine more completely the role that LD plays in the development of delinquent careers.

Besides informing the reader about the possible role of learning disabilities in the evaluation of delinquent careers, hopefully this paper has suggested the compatability of biological and sociological explanations of the etiology of juvenile delinquency. Here, data on learning disabilities was integrated into the Structural Functional perspective on delinquency, perhaps broadening its scope.

In conclusion, it should be noted that the early diagnosis of children with LD usually results in their being labeled as "special" and in their being assigned to "special classes." On the whole, this is probably a very positive process since it enables them to obtain needed help. However, there are those who have suggested that this labeling has a politics of its own which serves the needs of parents and educators rather than children (Schrag and Divoky, 1975). Furthermore, whether warranted or not, placement in a special education program does label a child as different and thus may subject him or her to unpleasant and perhaps unjust behavior at the hands of school authorities and "normal" peers. Hence, the subject of learning disabilities may also be applicable for integration in criminology's labeling perspective as well as into the Structural Functionalist perspective. But to accept the role of biological factors in the etiology of juvenile delinquency, sociological criminologists must become aware of their lack of intellectual peripheral vision which has caused them to ignore alternative explanations of criminal behavior.

REFERENCES

ACKERMAN, P. et al. (1977) "Teenage status of hyperactive and non-hyperactive learning disabled boys." American J. of Orthopsychiatry 47, 557.

BERMAN, A. (1975) "Incidence of learning disabilities in juvenile delinquents and non-delinquents: implications for etiology and treatment." Presented at 2nd International Scientific Conference, Brussels, Belgium, January 3-7, 1975.

BRUININKS, V. (1978) "Actual and perceived peer status of learning-disabled students in mainstream programs." J. of Special Education 12, 51.

CLOWARD, R. and L. OHLIN (1960) Delinquency and Opportunity. Glencoe, IL: Free Press.

COHEN, A. (1955) Delinquent Boys. New York: Free Press.

CRITCHLEY, M. (1972) The Dyslexic Child. London: William Heinemann Medical Books Ltd.

GILBERT, J. (1976) The Relationship of Cognitive Temp to Set, Behavior Problems, Intelligence and Achievement in Learning Disabled Elementary School Children. Ann Arbor, MI: University Microfilms International.

GROSS, M. and W. WILSON (1974) Minimal Brain Dysfunction. New York: Brunner/Mazel.

HUESSY, H. and A. COHEN (1976) "Hyperkinetic behaviors and learning disabilities followed over seven years." Pediatrics 57, 4.

HURWITZ, I., et al. (1972) "Neuropsychological function of normal boys, delinquent boys and boys with learning disabilities." Perceptual and Motor Skills 35, 3874.

LARSON, J. (1977) "Biological theories of criminality." University of Maryland. (unpublished)

MURRAY, C. et al. (1976) The Link Between Learning Disabilities and Juvenile Delinquency: Current Theory and Knowledge. Washington, DC: Government Printing Office.

PINCUS, J. and G. TUCKER (1974) Behavioral Neurology. New York: Oxford Univ. Press.

President's Commission on Law Enforcement and the Administration of Justice (1967) Task Force Report on Juvenile Delinquency and Youth Crime. Washington, DC: Government Printing Office.

SAFER, D. and R. ALLEN (1976) Hyperactive Children. Baltimore: University Park Press.

SCHRAG, P. and D. DIVOKY (1975) The Myth of the Hyperactive Child. New York: Pantheon.

SHAH, S. and R. LOREN (1974) "Biological and psychophysiological factors in criminality." In D. Glaser (ed.) The Handbook of Criminology. U.S.A.: Rand McNally.

VALETUTTI, P. (1975) "The teacher's role in the diagnosis and management of students with medical problems," pp. 1-14 in R. Haslam and P. Valetutti (eds.) Medical Problems in the Classroom. Baltimore: University Park Press.

Henry E. Kelly
University of Tulsa

6

BIOSOCIOLOGY AND CRIME

When most sociological treatises on crime, its causes, and its cures examine the "nature vs. nurture" controversy, they are content with an incomplete examination (e.g., Sutherland and Cressey 1970) which results in a negative evaluation of the contribution of biological causes. This is the result of seeing crime almost exclusively as a product of undersocialization or socialization to "unacceptable" values and norms, or pressuring external social structures, or simply free will choosing evil. The social psychological, social structural, and even moral viewpoints predominate. Thus, since crime is the result of behavior contrary to relativistic social norms, how then can biological causation be established?

It is my suggestion that we, as sociologists, should consider an alternate method of viewing crime. I suggest that we (a) consider some of the newer findings from biochemistry which may persuade us then to; (b) develop joint research projects with biochemists to see to what extent social and biochemical variables influence criminal behavior, especially the "irrational" type, such as alcohol or drug related or violent or impulsive crimes. Then, (c) *if* these biochemical causes actually are related to criminal behavior, we sociologists might want to see if they in turn have social causes; e.g., is an inherent biochemical condition also a result of socialization (one might think of cultural patterns of nutrition), or prevailing distributions of power or social structures (such as an economic system resulting in heavy metal poisoning or external pollution affecting internal biochemical environments). Is the internal biochemical environment of an individual a result of external social environments, or at the least modifiable by them? We have accepted as proper for sociological study the environment *external* to the human person; perhaps we now should consider appropriate the environment *internal* to the person, not just the social psychological environment but also the physical-biochemical environment. This paper suggests that it is inconsistent to consider social-psychological variables such as attitudes, opinions, feelings, and personality, and to neglect social-biochemical variables.

It is easy to understand this neglect when one briefly considers the inadequacy of past biological explanations. An example of a "constitutional" explanation is Lombroso's (1911) concept of the criminal as born thus and existing as an atavistic return to a primitive kind of man. His analysis of skulls and brains of criminals confirmed him in his conclusion that those of criminals are distinctively different. Sheldon (1949) and the Gluecks (1950) developed and tested somatotype theories stating a relationship between behavior and body structure.

Montagu's summary (1973) of studies of adult twins, both monozygotic and dizygotic, suggest a decisive influence of genetic factors. Finally, the studies by Jacobs (1965) lead him to see a relationship between an extra Y chromosome and aggressive behavior. A relationship between mental deficiency (inborn intellectual deficiencies) and crime was held by researchers such as Goddard (1920). A relationship betwen neurological functioning as measured by the EEG and crime is suggested by numerous researchers such as Stafford-Clark and Pond (1951).

The final category of supposed biological causation is that of endocrine abnormality. Schlapp (1928) estimated that one-third of prisoners suffered from toxic infection or glandular disturbance. Podolsky (1955) cited reports showing a relationship between hypolycemia and various types of crime. At this point, the critique by Nassi and Abramowitz (1976: 600) is noteworthy, although inadequate, as the rest of this article indicates.

> Thus, interpretations of criminality as manifestations of endocrine abnormality were not substantiated because: 1) conclusions were drawn from an institutionalized criminal population which constitutes a limited and selective group of criminals; 2) the physical condition of prisoners was subject to distortion by such special factors as poor diet, restricted physical activity, and unsanitary conditions; 3) normal physiological patterns subject to daily fluctuation were not demonstrated to be constant, so that the figures given by any single investigation were meaningless; and 4) it could just as easily have been argued that psychological dysfunction could lead to endocrine disfunction and, indeed, the effect of psychological stress upon glandular secretion is more widely documented than the reverse effect of glandular disturbance upon personality.

The sociological theories of crime causation are either social-psychological and centered on socialization and its internal social-psychological effects, or macro-structural and concentrated on social institutions and structures outside the individual.

One such difference is that between the functionalist school which tends to see crime as a result of inadequate socialization to cultural values and socially correct ways of behaving. Since society is based on an agreement among its members and its goals and its means of achieving them, behavior contrary to this is labeled deviant, and if serious enough it is sometimes labeled criminal. The inadequately socialized individual who has committed a crime and been apprehended is then processed through the criminal justice system and attempts are to be made to resocialize him.

Conflict theory, on the other hand, perceives much crime to be a rational or even necessary response to social structures of inequality which are discriminatory and unfair. The solution to crime certainly involves changing these structures, particularly the economic and political systems, to provide greater equality.

Biochemistry today offers us some provative studies which seem also to be interesting challenges as far as our topic is concerned. We will consider two general concepts and two specific areas. Consider first the concepts of biochemical individuality and orthomolecular medicine, and then the specific maladies, cerebral allergies, and inadequate sugar metabolism (hypoglycemia). It would have been quite appropriate to also include schizophrenia, but this would unduly lengthen this article.

As a basis for this biochemical approach is the concept of biochemical individuality (Williams, 1973, 1969). This concept states that we humans (as well as other organisms), though similar in our biological and biochemical composition, are absolutely unique; and, especially, that each biochemical composition has a pattern and distribution all its own. Newborn babies are remarkably different in the sizes of their internal organs. "Their circulatory and muscle system are various, their nerve patterns are unique, and their brain structures are highly distinctive in cellular makeup. The finger print and footprint differences . . . are inconsequential in comparison with these other aspects of hereditary difference" (Williams, 1973: 22).

Biochemical individuality is found in each human's individual need for the 40+ required nutrients for human life. Passwater (1976) summarizes Williams' argument against the validity of such a concept as the Recommended Dietary Allowance (RDA) of nutrients, e.g., vitamins, which are required by some average human beings. Taking only five nutrients, each with the amount necessary for a majority of adults, few of the adults would receive the amount they need. In this instance, the data would apply to only 3% of the adult population. The explanation is as follows:

449 out of 1,000 adults may require more of the first nutrient than that listed. Of the 501 remaining adults, 250 may need more of the second nutrient than the figure listed. With the third, fourth and fifth nutrients, 125, 62, and 31 additional individuals may be successively eliminated from the original 1,000 adults. The remainder is only 33 of the original 1,000 having their needs met by all five quantities of nutrients, say example had included a larger number of nutrients, say thirty, the number of people receiving the right vitamin quantities would be virtually zero. If, rather than calculating quantities required for the majority of adults (51 percent), one determined quantities to satisfy 80 percent of the adults, the collective estimates would apply to only one in 806 adults [Passwater 1976: 184].

Pauling (1976) points out that if we take 500 independently inherited characteristics, then there is only a 10% chance that one person in all the people in the world would be normal with respect to each of these 500 characters, i.e., would fall within the normal range (within which 95% of the values lie) in respect to each of these 500 characters. If we think of the some 100,000 characteristics that can actually vary, we see that no human being is "normal" in respect to each of these.

Further, these "abnormalities" spoken of above, which are part of biochemical individuality, can indeed be far outside the "normal" range. Pauling (1976) suggests that an optimum intake of ascorbic acid (vitimin C) for humans may vary over a forty-fold range from 250 mg. per day to 10 gr. per day, or an even wider range. Williams (1973, 1969) states that the available data show that in respect to individual needs for some amino acids and calcium, five-fold variations are by no means uncommon, that for vitamin A the variation may be ten-fold, and for vitamin D the need of one individual may be 2500 times the need of another.

These individual needs differences extend to most of the nutrients required by humans. Thus, the unique needs of individuals seem apparent and the ranges for these needs can indeed be quite large.

The concept of orthomolecular medicine flows from biochemical individuality and from the treatment of several human diseases by simply supplying one or more needed nutrients (which are actually human foods) in large, even very large, multiples of the average requirement. Pauling (1976) defines orthomolecular medicine as "the preservation of good health and the treatment of disease by varying the concentrations in the human body of substances that are normally present in the body and are required for health." For example, beriberi, scurvy, or pellagra can be prevented and treated by the intake of a certain amount of a vitamin unique to each of "these deficiency diseases." Only that vitamin and only the individually required amount will be successful.

The word orthomolecular comes from the Greek *orthos* and means the right or correct molecule (Fredericks, 1976). Orthomolecular medicine, then, sees much, perhaps most, disease as preventable and treatable by the proper diagnosis and supplementation of the biochemically individual need for the proper combination of the 40+ nutrients necessary for human life. Not only does this include a concern for additional amounts of needed nutrients to make the internal biochemical environment more ideal, but also necessitates the avoidance of any substances (the "wrong" molecule) which would bring on illness or preclude a cure. Examples of wrong molecules would be both substances which are not naturally found in the human body, and which are medically prescribed for relief of symptoms but not as cures of causes, e.g., tranquilizers, anti-depressants and pain-killers; and also substances which provide natural sustenance for many humans, but which provoke either allergic reactions (e.g., certain foods), or inappropriate endocrine reactions and biochemical depletion (e.g., refined sugar).

Very impressive examples of orthomolecular medicine are found in the field of psychiatry (Williams, 1973; Pauling, 1976; Passwater, 1976; Pfeiffer, 1975). One of the pioneers in this area was Abram Hoffer in Canada. In his practice, he noticed that many of the symptoms of schizophrenia were similar to those of pellagra, a niacin (B_3) deficiency disease. He then treated these patients with huge doses of vitamin B_3 and found that many patients recovered and remained non-schizophrenic as long as they contained these mega-vitamins doses. The disease was only "cured" as long as they continued their "abnormally" large doses of this vitamin, which for them was not an abnormal dose but rather a biochemically individualized and necessary amount. Since then, similar work by numerous psychiatrists (cf. Fredericks, 1976 and Pfeiffer, 1975) has shown that this type of therapy with niacin, ascorbic acid, pyrodozine (B_6), and other nutrients has assisted many patients for whom traditional talk-drug-shock treatment was of no avail.

Two other concepts remain to be treated before we consider the above information in relation to crime (and to sociology), and these are cerebral allergies and inadequate sugar metabolism (hypoglycemia). The subject of cerebral allergy is a topic of dispute among allergists. But many reputable medical doctors (e.g., Frazier, 1975 and Pfeiffer, 1975) present potent evidence in favor of the concept. Some symptoms associated with cerebral allergy (neural allergy) are "fatigue, nervousness, irritability, fears, rage, or the full panoply of perceptual distortions of time, sound, space, and reality which are characteristic of schizophrenia" (Fredericks, 1976: 30). This author further states that psychotic behavior has resulted from exposure to just one insecticide (which may be a drug effect rather than an allergic reaction).

Inadequate sugar metabolism (hypoglycemia) refers to the condition in which blood glucose levels are insufficient for proper brain and other body functioning. This area is important because of the importance of the brain for rationality and decisions, and since this organ, which weighs only

2-4% body weight consumes 25% of the body's glucose supply. Once again, this is an area of dispute among medical practitioners and biochemists. That hypoglycemia exists is admitted by all. That it is a relatively common disease probably caused or triggered by the inadequate and harmful eating habits of modern Americans is still disputed. Many medical professionals follow the lead of Seale Harris (who was both a hero and, later, not a hero for the American Medical Association) and view the American diet as responsible for a great number of hypoglycemics in the United States today. The symptoms of hypoglycemia can range from fatigue, headache, irritability, mental confusion and, dullness to rage, suicidal depression, and psychotic behavior (Pfeiffer, 1975; Fredericks, 1976).

Very briefly, we have considered the notions of biochemical individuality, orthomolecular medicine, cerebral allergy, and inadequate sugar metabolism (hypoglycemia). Now, what might these have to do with crime and with sociology? Considerable research in these areas by biochemists and medical researchers has presented us with plausible alternative explanations for much of human behavior which is labeled criminal, particularly the violent, the "irrational," and that related to alcohol or drug addiction or misuse. For instance, if a person is suffering severe and untreated hypoglycemia, it is conceivable that when his blood glucose level plummets, he may become enraged or psychotic and commit an irrational crime against a fellow human being. Episodes of rage and psychotic behavior are documented from the clinical practice of psychiatrists and other medical doctors when, in the administration of six-hour glucose tolerance tests, the blood glucose level falls precipitously (cf. Fredericks, 1976; Pfeiffer, 1975; Atkins, 1977). The hypoglycemic may suffer from temporary diminished responsibility because his brain could not function rationally, presenting alternatives among which he could actually choose. If this happens, and especially if it happens in many cases, the consequences of such a finding for the criminal justice system would be far reaching. Thomas Marsh (1977), Chief of Police of Fairfield, Ohio, cites the experiences of psychiatrists, R. Glen Green and Abram Hoffer, among others, who indicate that cerebral allergies and hypoglycemia can be causative factors in criminal behavior.

Fredericks (1977) cites a prison psychiatrist who stated in the May, 1976 issue of the International Academy of Preventive Medicine newsletter that prisoners showing the most clinical improvement from better nutrition have two characteristics. The first is an abnormal glucose tolerance test and the second is that they committed their offenses (murder, assault, rape) with impulsive violence and that before their nutrition was improved their behavior was impulsive, irritable, and combative. Fredericks (1977) also cited from the Journal of Orthomolecular Psychiatry in a 1975 article that states that a very large number of inmates suffer from hypoglycemia which "aggravates and perpetuates" criminal behavior. It goes on to suggest investigation of nutritional needs as "primary influences" in crime.

Ralph Bolton, an anthropologist, hypothesized hypoglycemia as a cause of the aggressive behavior of the Qolla in Peru. In one village of 1,200 persons half of the heads of households had been involved in homicide cases. The Qolla have one of the highest homicide rates in the world: 50 per 100,000. Bolton tested blood sugar levels and found them low in 50% of the people tested.

Irrational behavior brought about by deranged biochemistry is illustrated in the lists of symptoms associated with histapenic and histadelic patients (ones with excessively low or high blood and brain histamine levels). High levels of histamine are found in allergic persons.

> Histapenic patients . . . overstimulated . . . thoughts hurdling and somesaulting so rapidly through their distraught minds that ideation and speech processes become distorted and bizarre. Severe disperceptions . . . sensory, time, body, self and perception of others . . . fearful . . . Hallucinations . . .

audiences with disembodied voices . . . tyrannized by evil spirits. Histadelia . . . produces sucidal depression . . .disperceptions . . . often lose contact with reality . . . "blank mindedness," . . . Severe headache [Pfeiffer, 1975: 398, 399].

Alcohol and drug addiction seem to be related to much crime (Adams and Murray, 1973). That these two addictions are frequently related to unmet biochemically individual needs and to hypoglycemia seems probable from the studies of Williams (1973) and Pfeiffer (1975). Successful therapies were based on discovering the biochemical needs and supplementing them. Heroin or any drug overdoses can be neutralized with 30 to 50 grams of sodium ascorbate (a form of vitamin C) and heroin addiction can be overcome.

Cerebral allergies, since they directly affect the brain, can lead to psychotic behavior which conceivably could precipitate violent, irrational crime (Mandell, 1973; Philpott, et al., 1973; Challem, 1978).

David Hawkins, a psychiatrist, is doing research on "intractably violent patients" at the North Nassau Mental Health Center in Manhasset, New York. These violent patients have "quite a criminal arrest record for unprovoked assault." They have brain disrhythmia on an EEG and hypoglycemia. "They respond very positively. The program stops the violent, uncontrolled behavior" (Challem, 1978: 77). The therapy is based on the concepts of biochemical individuality and orthomolecular medicine.

It is important to emphasize that the "cures" in these areas of cerebral allergies and hypoglycemia are brought about primarily through biochemical changes in the natural constituents of the human body, *not* through psychological techniques, which have proven less than fruitful in these cases.

We have briefly examined the concepts of biochemical individuality, orthomolecular medicine, cerebral allergies, and inappropriate sugar metabolism from the field of biochemistry. Then some evidence for cerebral allergies and hypoglycemia and other biochemical disorders arising from individually unique needs as causative factors in violent and irrational human behavior and in alcohol and drug addiction was discussed. The evidence is not yet conclusive. The official positions of the American Medical Association and the American Psychiatric Association are generally opposed to the above interpretations (Atkins, 1977; Fredericks, 1976). They view with skepticism the claims of orthomolecular medicine in opposition to their use of therapeutic substances not found in normal human metabolism, e. g., prescription drugs. They reject orthomolecular psychiatry and prefer talk therapy, drug, and shock treatments.

But the above biochemical findings support some biochemical causation of violent and irrational behavior, in addition to alcohol and drug addiction, all of which are often associated with crime. With this kind of research continuing and with evidence of biochemical causation of some crime increasing, what should be the position of sociologists and criminologists who study crime?

C. Ray Jefferey (1977: 284) states that professional criminologists should have dropped "anomie, opportunity structure, differential association, social learning theory, conflict theory, and labeling theory" twenty years ago. He states that the genetic basis for aberrant behavior, including crime, has been demonstrated. He also cites the role of neurotransmitters as responsible for schizophrenia, alcohol and drug addiction, and other disordered behavior. He notes that in Cuyahoga Falls, Ohio, the probation department screens offenders for hypoglycemia. He suggests an interdisciplinary effort, primarily of the social sciences together with biology (which cooperation seems to refute his earlier call to discard sociological and psychological theories *in toto*).

I suggest that Jefferey has a point. We in Sociology, in our study of crime and of other deviant behavior, must not ignore these findings, particularly, from the field of biochemistry. These findings indicate that none of our social science explanations, singly, or in combination, will explain fully these behaviors—perhaps they can never explain more than a small part. It seems, then, an opportune time to join with biochemists in our research on crime (and deviant behavior) to develop together a more complete theory of human behavior. In fact, this kind of complimentary research may be as necessary for biologists and biochemists as for us; it may cause us to avoid the unverified over-simplification of the claims of some socio-biologists.

Finally, further study on our part to discover how social causes influence the internal biochemical environment seem to be called for. Obviously, social class influences the kinds of food one eats and access to knowledge which one can use to alter one's internal environment, e.g., through the findings of orthomolecular medicine. This genetotrophic concept (Williams, 1973), you recall, states that many of these biochemical abnormalities are predispositions to behave in certain ways, which can often be corrected chemically by supplying abnormally large amounts of natural nutrient substances. It seems that a theory of inequality could have a theoretical relationship with biochemical causes of criminal behavior. For those who profess elite theory, Marxism, et similia, a sadly curious reality may actually prevail in regard to social control in societies of inequality. It may well be that manipulative efforts controlled by elites in the socialization process may be far more effective than we have imagined. Much crime and deviant behavior may actually be caused biochemically and thus be truly irrational unresponsible behavior. It may be that as the biochemical causes are found and treated most all citizens would see the goals and means and rewards and punishments provided by advanced capitalist societies to be sufficient for them to conform. Thus, the problem may not be the coming large-scale biochemical control of a population, but the discovery that it is only needed on a very small scale—and under the legitimation of health and happiness and respectability by natural means. The prospect, if verified, might show us to be much closer to 1984 than we thought we were.

REFERENCES

ADAMS, R. and F. MURRAY (1973) Megavitamin Therapy. New York: Larchmont.

ATKINS, R. C. (1977) Dr. Atkins Super Energy Diet. New York: Crown.

BOLTON, R. (1974) Aggression in Qolla Society. Palo Alto, CA: National.

CHALLEM, J. J. (1978) "Vitamins and psychiatry." Bestways 6 (April): 77-78.

FRAZIER, C. C. (1975) Coping with Food Allergy. New York: Quadrangle.

FREDERICKS, C. (1977) "Hotline to health." Prevention 30 (Jan.): 44-50.

——— (1976) Psycho-Nutrition. New York: Grosset & Dunlap.

GODDARD, H. H. (1920) Human Efficiency and Levels of Intelligence. Princeton, NJ: Princeton Univ. Press.

GLUECK, S. and E. GLUECK (1950) Unraveling Juvenile Delinquency. New York: Commonwealth Fund.

JACOBS, J. A., et al. (1965) "Aggressive behavior, mental subnormality, and the XYY male." Nature 208: 1351-1352.

JEFFEREY, C. R. (1977) "Criminology—whither or wither?" Criminology 15 (Nov.): 283-286.

LOMBROSO, C. (1911) Crime, its causes and remedies. Boston: Little, Brown.

MONTAGU, A. (1973) An introduction to clinical ecology: allergic, ecologic and addictive factors in physical and mental disease. Presented to the International Academy of Metabology, March 23.

MARSH, T. O (1977) "Aggression and diet." Bestways (Nov.): 32-33.

NASSI, A. J. and S. T. ABRAMOWITZ (1976) "From phrenology to psychosurgery and back again. Biological studies of Criminality," Amer. J. of Orthopsychiatry, 46 (Oct.): 591-607.

PASSWATER, R. A. (1976) Supernutrition. New York: Pocket Books.

PAULING L. (1976) Vitamin, the Common Cold and the Flu. San Francisco: Freeman.

PFEIFFER, C. C. (1975) Mental and Elemental Nutrients. New Canaan, CN: Keats.

PHILPOTT, W. H., R. NIELSON and V. PEARSON (1973) (as quoted by Pfeiffer, 1975).

PODOLSKY, E. (1955) "The chemical brew of criminal behavior." J. of Criminal Law, Criminology and Police Sci. 45: 675-678.

SCHLAPP, P., and E. SMITH (1928) The New Criminology. New York: Lippincott.

SHELDON, W. H. (1949) Varieties of Delinquent Youth. New York: Harpens.

STAFFORD-CLARK, D. and D. D. POND (1951) "The psycopaths in prison: a preliminary report of a cooperative research." British J. of Delinquency, 2 (Oct): 117-129.

SUTHERLAND, E. and D. R. CRESSEY (1970) Criminology. New York: Lippincott.

WILLIAMS, R. J. (1973) Nutrition Against Disease. New York: Bantam.

——— (1969) Biochemical Individuality: The Basis for the Genotrophic Concept. Austin, TX: Univ. of Texas Press.

C. R. Jeffery
Florida State University

7

PUNISHMENT AND DETERRENCE
A Psychobiological Statement

The major argument of this essay is that any discussion of deterrence and punishment is impossible until a theory of behavior is put forth. Research in deterrence, thus far, is unclear and inconclusive due to the underlying assumptions about *behavior* which the researchers in the area have made. A major shift in paradigms must occur before a major theoretical system for deterrence can be suggested.

Recent reviews of deterrence research have concluded that the evidence concerning deterrence is mixed to say the least (Gibbs, 1975; Erickson et al., 1977; Geerken and Gove, 1977; Pontell, 1978; Blumstein et al., 1978). The arguments can be classified as follows:

(1) The statistical techniques are inadequate, do not take into account extralegal variables such as unemployment or social class, and do not allow for reciprocal or two-way causation (Pontell, 1978; Blumstein et al., 1978).

(2) The definition of punishment differs from that of deterrence, and punishment may affect the crime rate in ways other than through deterrence. Gibbs (1975) discusses nine such variables. Incapacitation has occupied a key role in such discussions (Geerken and Gove, 1977; Blumstein et al., 1978).

(3) The two-way causation model is critical when one views the effect of the criminal justice system on crime rates, as well as the effect of crime rates on the criminal justice

system. This problem has been referred to as system over-load (Geerken and Gove, 1977), system capacity (Pontell, 1978), and simultaneous effects (Blumstein et al., 1978). Although each of these authors writes as if he were alone in his observations, the point made is that the crime rate may influence the punishment response more than punishment influences the crime rate.

DETERRENCE AND PERCEPTION

The original statement on deterrence by Bentham assumed that deterrence was a psychological event to be explained by the hedonism of pleasure and pain. Sociologists, following Durkheim's dicta that there are no such things as biology or psychology, moved the issue of social control to the social level (Erickson et al., 1977). Social control became the restraining force of social norms and the internalization of social norms by individuals as moral obligations. This philosophy of human nature led to years of looking at group data and the effect of the death penalty in state A versus state B, or at time A versus time B.

Gibbs (1975) stated that deterrence was the omission of an act as a response to perceived risk of punishment. As such, deterrence is an unobservable phenomenon. *We never observe deterrence.* We assume deterrence from the absence of a response. This is an untestable proposition. As Gibbs observes, "regardless of what the individual does (commits or omits the act), it is not evidence of deterrence." As a result, deterrence research became a psychological approach through *perception.* This of course occurred mostly with sociologists who had neither the training nor interest in psychology needed to use a psychological model of behavior.

Claster (1967) was one of the early writers in the area of perception and deterrence. Henshel and Carey (Henshel and Silverman, 1975: 55-56) write that deterrence is a

PUNISHMENT ──────────► PERCEPTION ──────────► DETERRENCE

FIGURE 7.1

subjective perception which is in the eyes of the beholder. Deterrence thus becomes a state of mind or a mentalistic concept. Gibbs (1975) uses a model with perception acting as an intervening variable. Gibbs (1977: 419) says that "by definition no individual can be deterred unless he or she perceives the anticipated legal reaction to the crime as painful."

The move from deterrence to perception was an attempt to solve the impossible problem of measuring the nonexistent. In substituting perception for deterrence, the criminologists/sociologists created another major methodological issue: what is perception and where does it exist? As I have noted elsewhere (Jeffery, 1976; Jeffery, 1977) there are three basic models of behavior: mentalistic introspection, behaviorism, and biosocial behaviorism. The use of perception as an intervening variable between stimulus and response is mentalistic introspection.

Introspection is based on the dualism of mind v. body, nature v. nurture, materialism v. idealism, rationalism v. empiricism, free will v. determinism, values v. science, and genetics v. environment. It assumes a world of linear causation, a model for most behavioral science since the late nineteenth century (Klir, 1972: 25). Such a model of behavior divided the world into mind and matter, ideas and materials, with mind determining matter. Mind is a "black box" which is never directly observed but which is inferred from behavior. From behavior we infer such mental states as cognition, rationality, volition, and emotion, and then in turn we use our inferred conceptions to explain the behavior we observed in the first place. Mentalistic introspection uses one direct observation (of behavior) and two indirect

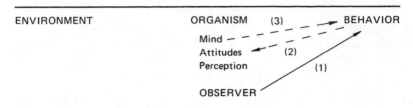

(1) Observation by the observer
(2) and (3) Inferences from behavior used to explain behavior

FIGURE 7.2

observations or inferences—mind and mind-causing behavior (see Figure 7.2).

The problem is obvious. The environment has an effect on the organism. The environment is internalized in the organism. The observer does not observe internal behavioral processes, he observes only external behavior. In order to link environmental experience to behavior the observer infers or imputes internal mentalalistic states which control behavior. But he never observes such internal mental states *independent of behavior.*

The way to get at internal states is through *introspection* (Brunswik, 1952; Zimbardo and Ruch, 1975). We ask people questions. We rely on verbal reports, interviews, and questionnaires. This is the so-called "survey method" so basic to sociology and criminology. Or we use the symbolic meanings within the individual. This led to participant observation and to psychoanalytic depth interviews. It is argued that verbal behaviors and test scores are not really behaviors but are a reflection of internal mental states. These internal states are often referred to as attitudes or perceptions.

For years social scientists have attempted to show a causal relationship between attitudes and behavior. In 1934, La Piere cast serious doubt on this proposition; he was followed by Westie and DeFleur, Deutscher, and Wicker (Schuman and Johnson, 1976). Wicker concluded that there was no evidence of a causal relationship between attitudes and behavior, or between verbal behaviors and other classes of behavior. The "attitudes cause behavior" argument used by most social scientists is another way of saying verbal behaviors cause other behaviors. Behavior cannot cause behavior. Behavior must be related to a variable (or variables) independent of behavior.

The field of environmental psychology is an attempt by psychologists to develop a model of behavior based on a man-environment model, with emphasis on the physical environment. The environment for the psychologist is physical, yet the organism is nonphysical. Between the organism and the environment the psychologist inserts perception, as in

environment   perception   organism.

Stokols (1977), from his review of the field of environmental psychology, states that the physical environment is mediated by perception, cognition, and learning (see also Stokols, 1978). Ittelson et al., (1974: 98) says that the critical process for man-environment interaction is *cognition*.

The basic research methods of environmental psychology are paper and pencil tests of attitudes, or what is often called cognitive mapping. As Michelson (1975) noted, perceptions, norms, and values are used to explain environmental psychology.

This still leaves us with the old dualism problem of how matter is transformed into mind, or how physical stimuli and environmental settings are transformed into attitudes and perceptions and cognitive maps. Barker (1968: 7), the ecological psychologist, stated that the core of the problem in environmental psychology is "how can psychology cope with nonpsychological inputs?" He is, of course, defining psychology as the logic of the psyche, which by definition is nonmaterial. Michaels (1974) wrote that "human ecology has been discussed in relation to the cognitive branch of psychology. The relation between ecology and the behavioral branch of psychology has apparently not been considered."

Whereas the environmental psychologist has tried to link a physical environment and a nonphysical organism, the sociologist has worked entirely on the nonphysical level for both environment and organism. The environment is social; the organism is social. As Duncan and Schnore (1959) observe, for the sociologist the relevant environment is the social environment which is conceived in terms of individual perceptions: "One searches the literature in vain for more than superficial reference to the brute fact that men live in a physical environment and that they employ material technology in adapting to it." Michelson (1976) notes that the social ecologist left the physical environment behind in the dust, while concentrating on the social environment.

Dunlap and Catton (1978), in a paper reviewing the theoretical structure of environmental sociology, state that environmental sociologists deal with the physical as well as the social environment. There is a recognition that a physical environment exists. They classify the individual's interaction with the environment as *physical and social,* but they concentrate on social interactions by means of symbolic meanings, attitudes, norms, and values. They retain the bifurcation of the world into physical and nonphysical. The social is nonphysical.

The use of attitudes and values as intervening variables between environment and organism is the heart of social psychology. As Manis (1978) notes, attitudes and beliefs are basic to sociological social psychology, though the relationship between attitudes and behavior is more complex than anticipated and it is practically impossible to predict behavior from knowledge of attitudes. He states that this type of psychology *assumes* that *verbal attitudes* are expressed as behavior patterns.

The separation of psychology and sociology was revealed in 1968 in the publication of the Handbook of Social Psychology edited by Lindzey and Aronson. Lindzey trained at Harvard under Parsons in social relations, and he is identified as a social psychologist. However, he is a psychological social psychologist who in recent years has published extensively in the area of behavioral genetics and biology. His view of psychology is totally foreign to sociologists, as seen in the reviews of his book by symbolic interactionists such as Stryker (1971) and Volkart (1971). Liska (1977) has discussed both the dissipation of social psychology (as now known to sociologists), and the challenges of a psychologically oriented social psychology.

As I have noted elsewhere (Jeffery, 1977: 102-103), Mead is regarded by sociologists as the father of symbolic interactionism. They take his book Mind, Self, and Society, and forget to read the part entitled "Mind" wherein he states that his psychology is called physiological psychology; there is a brain and neurons between a stimulus and a response. By "mind," Mead meant brain. Mead was forty years ahead of his time in his psychobiological approach to behavior, an approach totally ignored by symbolic interactionists.

In order to establish perception in deterrence research, college students are asked if they perceive risk of arrest or of criminal sanctions, e.g., "how likely are the police to catch you for the use of marihuana?" (Anderson et al., 1977; Waldo and Chiricos, 1972). In other words, we study the impact of pain on the organism by a verbal response to a questionnaire (see Figure 7.3). It should, of course, be obvious that one does not measure the impact of pain on behavior by measuring verbal responses to a questionnaire.

BEHAVIORAL PSYCHOLOGY
AND PUNISHMENT

Gibbs (1975: 219) concluded that we cannot test a theory of deterrence, and he then suggests that we look at the

ENVIRONMENT	ORGANISM	BEHAVIOR
Pain ──────────→	Perception ──────────→	Verbal Reports

FIGURE 7.3

consequences of punishment. Most of what we know about punishment from a scientific viewpoint originated in behavioral psychology and learning theory as found in Skinner. Behaviorism overcame the methodological issues involved in introspective psychology, and the use of indirect measures of behavior by refusing to deal with mentalistic concepts. Its framework is the association of a stimulus and a response on the basis of pain and pleasure, or punishment and reinforcement.

Punishment is defined as a consequence of behavior that reduces the future probability of that behavior (Azrin and Holz, 1966). By definition punishment works. In criminology we spend a great deal of time arguing whether or not it works, whereas by definition it works. All theories of learning are based on the general doctrine that man behaves so as to minimize pain and maximize pleasure. Two principles—pleasure and pain—are involved. Punishment is the pain side of the equation, that is, those sensations that an organism will avoid if at all possible.

I will not go into all of the reasons for the failure of punishment in the criminal justice system since they have been discussed in some detail elsewhere (Azrin and Holz, 1966; Jeffery, 1971; Jeffery, 1977). I want, rather, to discuss some of the basic features of punishment as it is related to behavior.

Skinner argues that punishment is most destructive of behavior and he advocates a system of rewards to motivate human behavior. His work challenges the basic tenets of our child rearing practices, educational policies, economic practices, and legal practices based on pain rather than pleasure. (The political implications of a pleasure-oriented psychology are yet to be developed and are for lack of space, merely suggested here.)

Punishment is maintained by its reinforcing qualities. It removes an aversive stimulus or it is rewarded with a reinforcing stimulus. Predatory aggression, for example, is maintained by the fact that it has survival value for the organism who is consuming another organism. We often exclude killing for food from our discussion of punishment.

Although punishment reduces the future response capability of the punished, it does so at a very high cost. Punishment creates anxiety reactions in the autonomic nervous system. Such anxiety is essential in learning to avoid punishing situations, and we shall return to this issue when we discuss the sociopath who cannot be conditioned to punishment. However, such anxiety states produce a high level of epinephrine in the brain, in interaction with the pituitary and adrenal glands, as well as with the autonomic nervous system. This is the so-called fight or flight response located in the hypothalamus and in the autonomic nervous system. Such stress and tension is basic to the so-called psychosomatic diseases such as ulcers, heart disease, high blood pressure, and so forth. Anxiety also interferes with learning new responses, and punishment is often more disruptive of behavior than it is helpful in establishing new response patterns.

Punishment also creates avoidance and escape responses (Azrin and Holz, 1966; Walter and Grusec, 1977; Newman, 1978). People do not learn to behave in a lawful way by being punished; they learn to avoid and escape punishment. The whole criminal justice system is the most beautiful example of escape and avoidance conditioning that one can imagine. We do not punish people into obeying the law; we condition them to avoid the police, to avoid arrest and prosecution, to plea bargain if arrested, to tell the judge and probation officer a fairy tale if convicted, and to make maximum use of the inmate subculture if sent to prison. A major industry called criminal justice is supported by the psychological principle that avoiding pain is reinforcing.

Avoidance and escape behavior can be most damaging to human relations, as for example when a student plays truant to avoid a punitive teacher, or a husband leaves home to avoid a nagging wife and child. The agent of punishment becomes a conditioned generalized aversive stimulus, and thus arouses all of the hostility, anger, anxiety, and escape behavior found in the original act of punishment.

Punishment creates anger and aggression in those punished. Azrin and Holz (1966) distinguish two types of pain-induced aggression. Operant aggression is aggression directed at the tormentor, an example of reinforcement through the removal of an aversive stimulus. We either escape from or attack our tormentor, much as a gentle gorilla will attack if burned with enough lighted cigarettes, or a dog will attack if teased.

In the annals of criminology one of the most consistent findings has been the lonely mass killer—the Charles Manson, the Charles Starkweather, or the Gary Gilmore. They come from homes without love or security, where beatings are everyday occurrences, where brutality is a way of life. Brutality begets brutality. Studies of child abuse show that the child abuser was an abused child. Manson made the classic statement in criminology when he noted that "you have created this garbage, and now you want to get rid of it." We take abused people who have been reared in punitive environments and subject them to more abuse in a jail and prison system. If I were asked to design an environment guaranteed to produce mean and vicious people, I would design an environment which looks like a prison system.

The brutalizing effect of punishment on the criminal justice system and on society has been a somewhat neglected part of deterrence studies, though Bowers and Pierce (1975) did publish a paper showing the increase in murder rates after an execution.

There is also elicited aggression (Azrin and Holz, 1966), that is, the general striking out of an organism that is in pain, as for example, the "kick the cat" syndrome or "go home from the office and take it out on the wife" syndrome. Pain produces aggression. This should give us a clue to the violence associated with the ghetto on a hot July evening, or the mass murderer who suddenly strikes out against society, as did Charles Whitmore from the tower of the University of Texas Library. Whitmore had a tumor the size of an egg in the amygdala area of the brain (the aggression center) and he was in constant pain for years before his violent episode.

Another harmful aspect of punishment is what Seligman (1975) calls *helplessness*. If an organism is placed in a position where escape or avoidance of pain is impossible, and where he has lost control over his environment, then a state of depression and helplessness occurs, often leading to serious physical deterioration or death. Learned helplessness is a major dimension of the practice of punishing individuals, especially children or those who are in institutions and have no means of escape other than suicide or psychosis.

Early in this discussion of punishment I noted that punishment was reinforcing to the punisher. This neglected aspect of punishment has been pursued especially by Zimbardo, the Stanford University social psychologist who did the mock prison studies with college students as guards and inmates. Zimbardo asks the question why we are so punitive in our social control methods. Why do people use punishment rather than reinforcement or restructuring the environment when they control the behavior of other people (Zimbardo and Ruch, 1975: 121; Jeffery, 1977: 283)?

Punishment is reinforcing to the punisher because it gives the punisher control and power over another person. It also acts as negative reinforcement by removing an aversive stimulus. Beating a child to death because it is crying is an effective way to remove a painful stimulus. We can remove the aversive stimulation produced by the criminal by placing him in prison or executing him. The removal of the criminal from society is reinforcing to those doing the removing. It does not reduce the crime rate in the future, and in fact may increase the crime rate, but it is nevertheless reinforcing. One of the major unasked questions in criminology is not what impact punishment has on the punished, but rather what impact does punishment have on those doing the punishment. Why is it that most of our citizens are in favor of the death penalty? Why do we elect people to high political office if they promise more executions? Why is it that any thread of evidence that punishment deters is picked up and used by the Supreme Court to justify brutality? Why do judges make pronouncements from the authority of the bench on the desirability of putting people to death? The deep-seated need for revenge must be sought in the structure of human nature, and in the fact man derives great pleasure from the suffering of others.

What I am saying is that the use of punishment by parents, teachers, lovers, husbands, wives, judges, and rulers has nothing whatsoever to do with whether punishment is effective in controlling the behavior of those punished. Punishment is used because it is *effective in controlling the behavior of the punishers.* Durkheim concluded that punishment was a social means of boundary maintenance, a means of reaffirming the collective conscience and moral fabric of society. Walters and Grusec (1977: 253) conclude from their review of punishment that "punishment will always be a necessary tool of behavior change."

On the other hand Azrin, an authority on punishment, concludes that "the disruption of social behavior constitutes the primary disadvantage to the use of punishment" (Azrin and Holz, 1966: 443). The evidence I have reviewed certainly supports Azrin's conclusions and raises serious doubts concerning the validity of the statement by Walters and Grusec, especially if we are talking about the severe forms of punishment found in the criminal justice system.

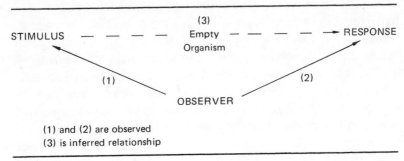

(1) and (2) are observed
(3) is inferred relationship

FIGURE 7.4

If we are to conclude that punishment must always be a necessary tool of behavior change, we had better do so on the basis of what it does for the punisher, and not what it does for the "punishee."

BIOLOGICAL BEHAVIORISM

The problems encountered in the analysis of behavior are primarily due to the "black box" created between the environment and the organism—or stimulus and response. The operant psychologist, following Skinner, dealt with an empty organism or "black box" concept of man (see Figure 7.4).

The link between response and stimulus is inferred in operant psychology, since the investigator does not know what happens to a stimulus once it enters the sensory system of the organism.

This type of psychology does away with mentalistic introspection, but it also does away with behavioral genetics and neurological functioning. Behavioral genetics developed out of a combination of chemistry and biology, then psychobiology came into existence in the 1960s as a result of the joining of biology and psychology (see Figure 7.5).

Today, learning is regarded as a psychobiological process involving the brain and nervous system. As Pribram (1969:

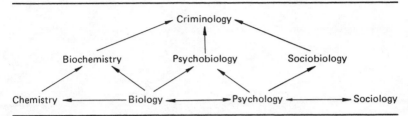

FIGURE 7.5

1) noted, learning theory is in a new phase, taking its cues from biology and declaring its independence from behaviorism which denounced or ignored biology. The new model of learning places a brain in place of the mind and uses observable neural functioning in place of verbal reports of attitudes and perceptions (see Figure 7.6).

Discussions of learning as a biological process can be found in Pribram (1969), Pribram (1971), Hilgard and Bower (1975), Hinde and J. Stevenson-Hinde, (1973) and Seligman and Hager (1972).

The basic differences in assumptions between a mentalistic introspective model and a biological behavioral model are as follows:

(1) The mind/body dualism is refuted and replaced with a physical model of the organism in which the brain replaced the mind.

(2) The organism/environment dualism or nature v. nurture argument is replaced with a genetic/environment interaction model. The old model is Vp = KgxVe, or variation in phenotype is a product of variation in the environment, with genetic differences being constant. The new model is Vp = VgxVe, or variation in phenotype is a product of variation in the genotype in interaction with variation in environment. It is not environment *or* genetics, but environment interacting *with* genetics.

(3) The argument for equipotentiality, that is, everyone is identical except for environmental differences, or each indi-

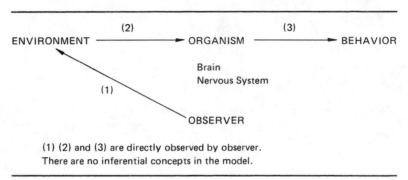

(1) (2) and (3) are directly observed by observer.
There are no inferential concepts in the model.

FIGURE 7.6

vidual has the same potential to learn from experience, is replaced with a doctrine of individual differences. No two individuals are alike except for identical twins.

(4) Environmentalism is replaced with biosocial learning theory, that is, learning is based on both the environment and the physical structure of the organism.

(5) The organism is biosocial, not social; physical, not mentalistic.

(6) The environment is physical, and not social, that is, the environment we call social is as physical as that environment we call physical.

(7) Age, sex, race, and urban areas are biosocial variables, not social variables.

(8) Adaptation of the organism to the environment is a physical process involving learning and behavior. The two important processes in human adaptation are learning and behavior.

We can compare the three models of behavior by the linkages between stimuli and responses (see Figure 7.7).

PLEASURE, PAIN, AND LEARNING

The brain is designed to receive information from the environment (see Figure 7.8), encode and store information, associate information with past information (memory and

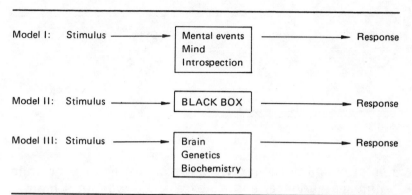

FIGURE 7.7

learning), and decode information through the motor system to control the stimulation of muscles (behavior).

The brain has four major divisions and functions: (1) sensory; (2) motor; (3) motivation and emotion; and (4) association and control. The brain is capable of storing past information (memory and learning) and making use of such information for future behavioral responses. Learning consists of changes in the biochemical codes of the neurons. A change in code results in a change in behavior (see Figure 7.9).

Learning is a combination of genetic and environmental inputs. Since statements about punishment and deterrence are statements about learned behavior, it is essential that we base our theory of punishment on a theory of learning. This has been ignored in the deterrence research cited at the beginning of this paper.

What is learned is a combination of genetic predisposition or genetic preparedness to learn (Seligman and Hager, 1972) in interaction with environmental experiences. The environment can have no impact on an organism devoid of genetics and a brain. The impact of sensation on behavior depends entirely on the structure of the brain. The environment produces no responses in an organism; only excita-

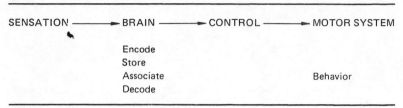

SENSATION ————→ BRAIN ————→ CONTROL ————→ MOTOR SYSTEM

Encode
Store
Associate   Behavior
Decode

FIGURE 7.8

tion of neural tissue produces responses. There is no brain without experience, and no experience without a brain.

The brain stands between stimulus and response, and it interprets the stimulus as pleasurable or painful. Punishment is a function of the brain. The stimulation of certain types of neural tissue is intepreted by the brain as pain, that is, the brain must act to remove or to reduce the source of the stimulation. By definition pain is stimulation which is turned off by the brain.

In recent years it has been discovered that pleasure and pain centers are located in the hypothalamus or emotional and motivational centers of the brain (Berlyne and Madsen, 1973: Carlson 1977: 471). Motivation and emotion are closely related to the pleasure and pain centers of the brain. It has been hypothesized that schizophrenics are lacking in a biochemistry associated with the pleasure centers of the brain.

Another major breakthrough in brain chemistry occurred with the discovery of endorphin. Endorphin is a natural opiate produced by the brain and pituitary gland in interaction which acts to block stimulation of neural sites in the brain related to pain (Villet, 1978; Snyder, 1977). The discovery of opiate receptors and natural opiates in the brain has raised new possibilities for the treatment of schizophrenia and drug addiction through biochemistry. Mental illness today is regarded as a biochemical disorder of the brain, and many successful therapies are based on the biochemical structure of the brain (see Figure 7.10).

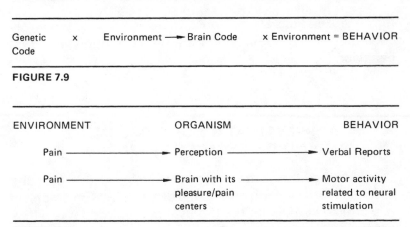

Genetic   x   Environment ——► Brain Code   x Environment = BEHAVIOR
Code

FIGURE 7.9

ENVIRONMENT	ORGANISM	BEHAVIOR
Pain ——————————►	Perception ————————►	Verbal Reports
Pain ——————————►	Brain with its ————► pleasure/pain centers	Motor activity related to neural stimulation

FIGURE 7.10

Let me now compare the *perception model* of deterrence with the *biosocial model.* Pain may arouse verbal behavior, but the important motor activities are not those associated with verbalization, but with removing the painful stimulus. We cannot measure the impact of pain on behavior by asking people to verbalize about it.

The major connection between brain chemistry and criminology comes in the area of sociopathy. For years Eysenck, Trasler, Hare and others have investigated the inability of certain organisms to condition to punishment, a condition known as sociopathy. One interpretation of this condition is based on Mowrer's work on conditioned emotional responses and the state of anxiety produced by the threat of punishment. This conditioning process operates through the hypothalamus and autonomic nervous system. Sociopaths are the opposite of schizophrenics: They are underaroused and understimulated and therefore do not experience or respond to the threat of pain by escape or avoidance responses. Recent books by Mednick and Christiansen (1977), Eysenck (1977), and Hare and Schalling (1978) have reviewed in detail the literature on sociopathy. The theoretical interpretation of sociopathy is still under development, but the implications for punishment and deterrence research are obvious: There is a major biological condition which totally alters the effect of punishment on behavior.

A RE-EVALUATION OF PUNISHMENT AND DETERRENCE RESEARCH

This brings me to my major conclusion concerning the psychobiology of punishment and deterrence. The organism is a critical variable in the theory. Each individual is different in brain structure, past experience, genetic inheritance, and present environmental conditions. If we ask the simple question whether or not punishment works, the answer is "under what conditions and for what individuals?" The impact of a painful stimulus on a male will depend on his testosterone level, among other things. The impact of stimulation on a female will differ depending on the menstrual cycle. A person who has experienced pain and frustration all of his life will behave differently than one who has not. One set of genes and experiences produces a different response to punishment than another set of genes and experiences. The impact of a stimulus on a response depends on (1) the past genetic history of the species and of the individual under study; (2) the past conditioning history of the individual; (3) the present state of interaction of organism and environment; and (4) the future contingencies attached to response patterns.

Punishment and deterrence can only be understood with an interdisciplinary theory of behavior based on biology, psychology, and sociology. The major components of such a theory involve behavioral genetics and psychobiology. This adds up to a theory of learning. Behavior is learned. Deterrence theory attempts to explain how individuals learn to avoid certain stimuli. Learning is a biochemical code in the brain. We are deterred if the proper code is in the brain.

The implications of brain research for criminology are great. We might begin by discussing why behavior control systems are a failure, and why most actions taken to suppress crime in fact increase crime. It means we cannot do deterrence research oblivious of the individual organism involved in punishment, be it the punisher or "punishee." We cannot ask if fixed sentences, longer sentences, or the death penalty deter. We must be aware of the fact that the effect of punishment on an organism is a most complex biosocial process. No two organisms are the same, no two environments are the same.

What this all suggests is a totally different model of behavior, and a totally different methodology for studying behavior. We must move beyond perception and survey data and verbal reports as measurements of environmental impact on behavior. We must develop the capability for tracing a painful stimulus into the organism to the associational and motivational areas of the brain and then to the motor centers and to behavior. Between the stimulus and the response is a great big black box. I will not now suggest that within this black box lie the answers to the riddle of behavior. But I will suggest that it is here that we will find the questions we should be asking about behavior.

REFERENCES

ANDERSON, L. S., T. CHIRICOS, and G. P. WALDO (1977) "Formal and informal sanctions: a comparison of deterrent effects." Social Problems 25 (October): 103-114.

AZRIN, N. and W. C. HOLZ (1966) "Punishment," in W. K. Honig (ed.) Operant Behavior: Areas of Research and Application, New York: Appleton-Century-Crofts.

BARKER, R. (1968) Ecological Psychology. Stanford: Stanford Univ. Press.

BERLYNE, D. E. and K. B. MADSEN [eds.] (1973) Pleasure, Reward, and Preference. New York: Academic Press.

BLUMSTEIN, A., J. COHEN, and D. NAGIN [eds.] (1978) Deterrence and Incapacitation: Estimating the Effects of Criminal Sanctions on Crime Rates. Washington, DC: National Academy of Sciences.

BOWERS, W. J. and G. L. PIERCE (1976) "Illusion of deterrence in Ehlick's research on capital punishment." Yale Law J. 85: 187-208.

BRUNSWIK, E. (1952) The Conceptual Framework of Psychology. Chicago: Univ. of Chicago Press.

CARLSON, N. R. (1977) Physiology of Behavior. Boston: Allyn and Bacon.

CLASTER, D. S. (1967) "Comparison of risk perception between delinquents and nondelinquents." J. of Criminal Law, Criminology and Police Science 58 (March): 80-86.

DUNCAN O. D. and L. F. SCHNORE (1959) "Cultural, behavioral, and ecological perspectives in the study of social organization." Amer. J. of Sociology (September): 132-146.

DUNLAP, R. and W. R. CATTON , Jr. (1978) "Environmental sociology: a framework for analysis." Paper presented at the annual meeting of the Society for the Study of Social Problems, September.

ERICKSON, M. L., J. P. GIBBS, and G. F. JENSEN (1977) "The deterrence doctrine and the perceived certainty of punishment." Amer. Soc. Rev. 42 (April): 305-317.

EYSENCK, H. J. (1977) Crime and Personality. 3rd ed. London: Routledge and Kegan Paul.

GEERKEN, M. and W. R. GOVE (1977) "Deterrence, overload, and incapacitation: an empirical evaluation." Social Forces 56 (December): 424-447.

GIBBS, J. P. (1977) "Social control, deterrence, and perspectives on social order," Social Forces 56 (December): 408-423.

——— (1975) Crime, Punishment and Deterrence. New York: Elsevier.

HARE, R. D. and D. SCHALLING (1978) Psychopathic Behavior. New York: John Wiley.

HENSHEL, R. L. and R. A. SILVERMAN (1975) Perception in Criminology. New York: Columbia Univ. Press.

HILGARD, E. and G. BOWER (1975) Theories of Learning. Englewood Cliffs, NJ: Prentice-Hall.

HINDE, R. A. and J. STEVENSON-HINDE (1973) Constraints on Learning. New York: Academic Press.

ITTELSON, W. H., H. M. PROSHANSKY, L. C. RIVLIN, and G. H. WINKEL (1974) An Introduction to Environmental Psychology. New York: Holt, Rinehart, & Winston.

JEFFERY, C. R. (1977) Crime Prevention Through Environmental Design (rev. ed.) Beverly Hills, CA: Sage.

——— (1976) "Criminal Behavior and the Physical Environment." Amer. Behavioral Scientist 20 (November-December): 149-174.

——— (1971) Crime Prevention Through Environmental Design. Beverly Hills, CA: Sage.

KLIR, G. [ed.] (1972) Trends in General Systems Theory. New York: John Wiley.

LISKA, A. D. (1977) "The dissipation of sociological social psychology." Amer. Sociologist 12 (February): 2-8.

MANIS, M. (1978) "Cognitive social psychology and attitude change." Amer. Behavioral Scientist 21 (May-June): 675-690.

MEDNICK, S. and K. O. CHRISTIANSEN (1977) Biosocial Bases of Criminal Behavior. New York: Gardner.

MICHALS, J. W. (1974) "On the relation between human ecology and behavioral social psychology." Social Forces 52 (March): 313-316.

MICHELSON, W. H. (1976) Man and His Urban Environment: A Sociological Approach. Reading, PA: Addison-Wesley.

——— (1975) Behavioral Research Methods in Environmental Design. New York: John Wiley.

NEWMAN, G. (1978) The Punishment Response. Philadelphia: J. P. Lippincott.

PONTELL, H. (1978) "Deterrence: theory v. practice." Criminology 16 (May): 3-22.

PRIBRAM, K. H. (1971) Languages of the Brain. Englewood Cliffs, NJ: Prentice-Hall.

——— [ed.] (1969) On the Biology of Learning. New York: Harcourt, Brace Jovanovich

SCHUMAN, H. and M. P. JOHNSON (1976) "Attitudes and behavior," in A. Inkeles (ed.) Annual Review of Sociology. Palo Alto: Annual Reviews.

SELIGMAN, M.E.P. (1975) Helplessness. San Francisco: W. H. Freeman.

——— and J. HAGER (1972) Biological Boundaries of Learning. New York: Appleton-Century-Crofts.

SNYDER, S. H. (1977) Opiate Receptors and Internal Opiates. Scientific American 236 (March): 44-56.

STOKOLS, D. (1978) "Environmental psychology," in M. Rosenzweig and L. Porter (eds.) Annual Review of Psychology. Palo Alto: Annual Reviews.

——— (1977) Perspectives on Environment and Behavior. New York: Plenum Press.

STRYKER, S. (1971) "Review of The Handbook of Social Psychology." Amer. Soc. Rev. 36 (October): 894-898.

WALDO, G. P. and T. G. CHIRICOS (1972) "Perceived penal sanction and self-reported criminality: a neglected approach to deterrence research." Social Problems 19 (Spring): 522-540.

WALTERS, G. P. and J. E. GRUSEC (1977) Punishment. San Francisco: W. H. Freeman.

VILLET, B. (1978) "Opiates of the mind." Atlantic 241 (June): 82-89.

VOLKART, E. (1971) "Review of Handbook of Social Psychology." Amer. Soc. Rev. 36 (October): 898-902.

ZIMBARDO, P. and F. L. RUCH (1975) Psychology and Life, 9th ed. Glenview: Scott Foresman and Co.

Fred Kort
University of Connecticut
Stephen C. Maxson
University of California

8

POLITICS IN A
BIOBEHAVIORAL PERSPECTIVE
A Report on a Course
Based on a New Paradigm

For several decades of the twentieth century, in an era
of immense expansion of the social sciences, biology
received little or no attention in these disciplines in general
and in political science in particular. Considering that no
human behavior, including—of course—political behavior,
would be conceivable without the central nervous system,
this neglect is surprising. Nevertheless, it is understandable
in view of the impact of Social Darwinism on political and
economic thinking in the United States and—with more
formidable consequences—on the development of totalitarian governments during the early part of this century.

Students of the social sciences are familiar with Herbert
Spencer's application of Darwinian ideas to the study of
social development. In a form that does not represent
Darwin's theory accurately, the concepts of "the struggle
for existence" and "the survival of the fittest" were applied
by Spencer to the social organism. On this basis, Spencer
argued in favor of a nonintervention of government in

AUTHORS' NOTE: Delivered at the 1978 Annual Meeting of the American
Society of Criminology, November 8-12, Dallas, Texas.

economic affairs, notably in his treatise *Man Versus the State* (1893). His ideas had a decisive influence in the United States at the beginning of the twentieth century, where it created a "new" philosophy of *laissez faire,* "new" because its foundations were different from the Lockean-Jeffersonian conception, which was based on "natural rights" in the sense of Stoic philosophy, and which had characterized American political thought more than a century earlier. That even a majority of Supreme Court justices was receptive to Spencer's ideas is evident from a dissent by Justice Holmes in a case in which the Court had declared unconstitutional a New York State law that had limited work hours in bakeries to ten hours per day and sixty hours per week (Lochner v. New York, 1905). Justice Holmes criticized the other justices on the Court for reading "Mr. Herbert Spencer's Social Statics" into the "due process" clause of the Fourteenth Amendment to the Constitution.

There were more horrifying consequences of Social Darwinism, however. Although neither Spencer nor his intellectual followers can be held responsible for such a development, Social Darwinism became an ideological component of National Socialism in Germany, with the result that genocide of several million persons was committed in the alleged interest of a "superior race."

Understandably, a pervasive aversion to doctrines based on distorted biology became prominent in the social sciences. The disregard of the biological foundations of human behavior (which indeed characterized the social sciences during the middle of the twentieth century) until a few years ago, was not justifiable, however, on the basis of the abuse of biology. Presumably, few social scientists would be satisfied with the assumption that *Homo sapiens* descended from Adam and Eve. Consequently, it may be prudent to consider evolution at least as an alternative hypothesis. It is with this recognition that a new orientation toward biology in the social sciences in general and in political science in particular emerged. This orientation is totally different from Social Darwinism with respect to its scientific foundations, as well as with regard to its normative aspects.

Undoubtedly, every student in the social sciences has been reminded many times that human behavior is complicated and that the difficulties in predicting it are immense. A simple biological fact would have been very instructive on this point. This fact is described in an admittedly speculative book by Carl Sagan (1977), which normally is not cited in scientific literature, although the fact itself is unquestionably scientifically valid and the author is an eminent scientist. He explains that the human brain consists of ten billion or 10^{10} nerve cells. Each of these cells has one to ten thousand links with adjacent nerve cells or 10^3 to 10^4 such links. If each link sends a yes-or-no message from one cell to another, the number of yes-no communications or such items of communications that the brain could contain would be $10^{10} \times 10^3 = 10^{13}$ or ten trillion items, if the lowest estimate for the number of links is used. Since there are two possible communications for each link, yes or no, the number of possible states of the human brain is (2^{10^3}). This number is larger than the total number of elementary particles (electrons and protons) in the entire universe, which is much less than (2^{10^3}). To be sure, many of these possible states never occur. Nevertheless, the number of configurations that do occur is enormous, and it thus is suprising that regularities in human behavior exist at all. Such a simple explanation of the difficulties of predicting the behavior of *Homo sapiens* would have been helpful in the social sciences a long time ago.

Actually, an orientation employing such explanations occurred only recently. Surely the changes in psychology —a discipline the impact of which on political science, as on the other social sciences, has been recognized for a long time—are decisive in this respect. As psychology has changed (i.e., the increasing orientation toward psycho-biology and the biobehavioral sciences in general), the form of this influence on political science understandably also has changed. Early indications, such as studies of the "authoritarian personality" and of the political beliefs of children, provided the initial signals for a new development, although they may not have been recognized as such. Then came developments that—in a most recent retrospective assessment by Peter Corning (1978)—have been called Biopolitics I and Biopolitics II.

Where does the new biological orientation in political science stand now? An appraisal by Albert Somit (1976: 5-7) identified four main components of this orientation:

(1) general considerations for a biologically oriented political science;
(2) insights from ethnology with respect to political behavior;
(3) physiological aspects of political behavior;
(4) public policy ramifications of the interface between biology and politics.

With modifications in terminology and respective emphases, the course under discussion has been organized on the basis of these components. The participants in the course are Victor Denenberg, Hana Dolezalova, Benson Ginsburg, Albert Harper, and Stephen Maxson, in the Department of Biobehavioral Sciences at the University of Connecticut, and Elizabeth Hanson, Norman Kogan, Fred Kort, Max Thatcher, Frederick Turner, and Jean Yarbrough, in the Department of Political Science. Kort and Maxson assumed responsibility for organizing the course.

The limits of this presentation do not permit a detailed description of the course. Nevertheless, an attempt will be made to indicate its main parts, to identify the topics of each part, and to explain why these topics were chosen. The preceding remarks already directed attention to the first part of the course, *Conceptual Framework for Inquiry*, including the topics "Principal Questions and Issues" and "Biological and Nonbiological Models." The remarks that follow will be devoted to the three other parts. With respect to all parts, the correspondence to the components identified by Somit (1976) should be noted again.

THE NATURE OF HOMO SAPIENS AND ITS IMPACT ON POLITICAL BEHAVIOR AND INSTITUTIONS

The convergence of biology and the study of politics was apparent many centuries before the emergence of biology as a modern science. The importance of the nature of man for an understanding of political institutions was clearly recognized in the philosophies of Plato and Aristotle, and undoubtedly even in much earlier times. Before examining the nature of *Homo sapiens* in terms of modern biology, therefore, it is proper to address oneself to "The Issue in the Context of Political Thought." Max Thatcher's presentation of this topic in the course makes clear that the questions pertaining to the origin and the function of the state in relation to the nature of the individuals who constitute this political entity are recurrent themes in the theories of Plato, Aristotle, Machiavelli, Hobbes, Locke, Rousseau, Kant, Hegel, Bentham, James and John Stuart Mill, Marx, Spencer, and Pareto—to name only a few, from different centuries, and similar as well as diverse sets of ideas. The perpetual question of the rationality or irrationality of man, and the corresponding requirements for government elicited conflicting views, as the thoughts of Locke and Rousseau in contrast to the ideas of Le Bon and Mac-Dougall, before the sophistication of contemporary psychology. Even conceptions of evolution, as Thatcher notes, could be found at least as early as the time of the Epicureans.

The nature of man as an "Issue in the Context of Special Cases in Political Philosophy," in the ideas of Hamilton,

Madison, and Jefferson, is discussed in Jean Yarbrough's course. Two main reasons for this special emphasis become apparent in Yarbrough's explanation of Federalist and Jeffersonian political thought. First, Hamilton, Madison, and Jefferson were in the unique position of being not only important political theorists, but also prominent statesmen whose thoughts and actions shaped the destiny of a polity. Although Hamilton and Madison did not think that human nature was "evil," they firmly believed in the need for effective institutional and procedural restraints on human action, such as checks and balances between the branches of government, which—in their various manifestations— are, of course, still a dominant characteristic of the American political process. Second, Jefferson's conception of human nature, which in its emphasis on benevolence certainly was different from the ideas of the Federalists, was not based only on traditional philosophy. Jefferson had a decisive interest in the natural sciences, he performed his own experiments, and he was prepared to give thought to a physiological basis of human behavior almost a century before Darwin.

With an example of convergence of traditional political philosophy and biological thinking, it is appropriate to turn to behavioral evolution. It would be difficult to make much progress in the discussion of this subject without at least some observations on genetics. For this reason, the first presentation in the course on the series of topics pertaining to evolution is given by Benson Ginsburg on "Genetic Aspects of Behavioral Evolution." Ginsburg makes the difference between preMendelian and postMendelian developments clear in his presentation, but he notes that conceptions that were advanced by Darwin and Galton still persist. Related to this observation should be the recognition that one explanatory system alone—such as Pavlovian psychology, psychoanalysis, Talcott Parsons' theories, or even sociobiology—cannot provide a pervasive view of human nature. Moreover, case studies and experimental evidence pertaining to the restoration of normal behavior in animals and humans have shown that there is much more flexibility in development than formerly was believed. One point on which Ginsburg is especially emphatic is that gene frequencies alone have explanatory value only within limits, which must be carefully recognized. It is in this connection that he notes the importance of reexamining the assumptions of sociobiology.

The explanatory potential of evolutionary theory with respect to behavior, as well as the necessary caution, also is reflected in the course by Maxon's presentations on "Comparative Aspects of Behavioral Evolution," the "Phylogeny of Behavior," and "Ecological Aspects." One approach to understanding the nature of man has been the investigation of similarities and differences between man and animal, and of their evolutionary bases. In the study of behavioral evolution, there are three key issues: What were the origins and changes for evolved behaviors, which behaviors were evolved adaptations to what environmental selection pressures, and what were the genetic bases for the evolution of behaviors? The last of these issues is considered in Ginsburg's lecture, and the first two are considered in Maxon's three presentations. These topics have been the concern of the disciplines of comparative psychology and of ethology, and they trace their beginnings to the writings of Darwin, especially Chapter VIII of *The Origin of Species* (1964), Chapters III and IV of *The Descent of Man* (1974), and all of *The Expression of Emotions in Man and Animals* (1965).

In *The Descent of Man,* Darwin argues that there is no fundamental difference in kind between the mind of man and of animals; that the mind of man and of animals can be represented as extreme points on a continuum; and that gradual changes can be traced from one group of animals to the next. This is the Hypothesis of Mental Continuity, first tested experimentally for cognitive processes in studies of associative learning in man and animals by E. L. Thorndike (1899). On the basis of these studies, he proposed that in all animals the intellect is a system of connections subject to the laws of exercise and of effect, and that the processes of learning are the same in crabs, fish, turtles, cats, dogs, and human infants. This hypothesis suggests that the evolution of mental capacity consists of quantitative changes in the ability to form associations between stimulus and response, and that species' differences in learned performance are due to differences in noncognitive traits, such as sensory responsiveness or motor capabilities. Until recently, this hypothesis was the predominant one in comparative psychology, and it was the basis of the belief that the study of learning in the white rat would lead to general laws of cognitive psychology applicable to all animals, including man. Since the Second World War, this hypothesis has been challenged by H. Harlow in comparative studies of learning sets, and by M. E. Bitterman in comparative studies of reversal and probability learning. Bitterman suggests that these studies on fish, turtles, pigeons, rats, and monkeys are consistent with a hypothesis of general and unique laws of learning, and that the unique laws are associated with changes in phylogenetic grade. Maxson uses these studies to illustrate the conceptual and methodological problems involved in controlling irrelevant variables in comparative studies of learning, and in inferring that similar or different mental processes underlie similar or different performance on the same task. He also suggests that similar concerns must be considered in applying the comparative approach to political science and to comparative studies of human aggression and altruism.

The origins of "ethology" may be traced to Chapter VIII of *The Origin of Species*, and to *The Expression of Emotions in Man and Animals*. In these works, Darwin emphasizes the differences among animals, and between animals and man, rather than the similarities presented in *The Descent of Man*. Ethology is also concerned with the evolutionary history and adaptive significance of behavioral differences between species. In his second presentation, Maxson describes the classical theory of ethology developed by K. Lorenz (1971) and N. Tinbergen (1951) concerning the immediate causes of behavior. By definition and example, the concepts of appetitive behavior, taxes, consummatory behavior, fixed action pattern, sign stimuli, innate releasing mechanism, and action specific potential are described. Maxson emphasizes that the classic theory was a useful model, that it had undergone considerable modification and revision, and that he is presenting it as background for a consideration of the ethologists' methods and conclusions in studying the phylogeny (origin and change) of displays or social releasers. Most of these studies have used insects, fish, and birds, and have focused on courtship or aggressive behaviors. Maxson suggests that these studies depend on the validity of applying the concept of homology to behavior. In evolutionary theory, two behaviors in different species would be homologous if they were derived from the same behavioral trait in a common ancestor. Recently, J. W. Atz (1970) has argued that the criteria used to assess whether two behaviors in different species are homologous are either difficult to apply in reality or invalid not only for behavioral but also for other traits, and that consequently it is difficult, if not impossible, to trace the evolutionary origin and history of motor patterns serving as social releasers. Maxson also emphasizes that this issue is by no means resolved and suggests that it must be considered in applying comparative or evolutionary approaches to considerations of the phylogeny of human behavior and of problems in political science.

Behaviors in two species may be similar because they are homologous and trace their similarity to a common ancestor, or because they are analogous and trace their similarity to common environmental selection pressures acting on unrelated lineages. Difficulty in differentiating similarity due to common ancestry and to convergent evolution is one of the reasons that it may be virtually impossible to trace the evolutionary origins and histories for behavior. However, convergent evolution of behavior traits may be used to determine what were the environmental selection pressures acting to bring about a behavioral adaptation.

In his third presentation, Maxson considers the issues of adaptive significance of behavior and of the environmental selection pressure leading to the behavioral adaptations. This is also a topic considered by Darwin and by the ethologists. Maxson first reviews the central thesis of evolutionary theory that differential reproductive selection of heritable variants leads to adaptation. Examples are given for the evolution of adaptive reproductive behaviors of birds and social behavior adaptations of carnivores. Difficulties inherent in the conceptual and methodological application of this approach are also discussed. Again, Maxson suggests that attempts to determine the selective advantage of human behavioral adaptation must be approached with an understanding of the limitations of comparative and ecological studies, and that applications of such findings to human behavior must be critically evaluated before relating them to issues in political science.

On the basis of the general considerations of evolutionary theory of behavior advanced by Ginsburg and Maxson, Albert Harper addresses himself specifically to "Primate Evolution and Behavior," "Human Evolution," and "Being Human." That primate behavior is of particular interest to the study of political behavior in human societies already can be inferred from the attention Maxson directs to the concept of homology, although it has been seen that he introduces the applicability of this concept to the study of behavior with all proper caution. By providing a basic familiarity with primate taxonomy, Harper sets the background for evaluating adaptations and behaviors in different primate genera. In this connection, he also offers a review of primate locomotion and adaptation to different niches. Primate social organization in its various forms among terricolous and arboreal primates then is described in his presentation. Aspects of the biology of social life, with respect to canine teeth and maternal care in particular, as well as with regard to genetic consequences of social life in general, are examined by Harper and lead to the following important questions in the discussion: Why do we study primates? Are they really good models for studying humans? These questions are especially pertinent for the study of political behavior. It will be noted in a moment that, in his third presentation, Harper emphasizes that 99% of human history is the history of hunting societies. In this respect, therefore, do not canids actually provide better models for the study of human social organization than primates?

A brief review of evolutionary motivation is the introduction to Harper's second presentation, devoted to human evolution. Clearly, methodological considerations become important in this context. Thus the time and circumstances of the major fossil remains are reviewed, physical characteristics are examined, and inferences on the behavior and social organization of each group are attempted, to provide some insights on the following questions: Is Ramapithecus our Miocene ancestor or another ape? Is Australopithecus man-ape or ape-man? What do we know about *Homo erectus*? Is there any further elucidation of the Neanderthal problem?

As has been indicated, in his third presentation Harper devotes special attention to the nature, complexity, and biology of hunting, a phenomenon that—in view of its impact on human development—deserves the name "Master Biobehavioral Complex." Equal emphasis in this presentation is given to species diversity and the arrival of modern man, and the following salient question is raised: Are the differences between modern populations significant? A discussion of the correspondence of culture and biology as a guide to the pathways of an attuned existence (adaptation) follows, and the biological future of *Homo sapiens* then is considered in terms of the decisive questions of ethnic identity and immense population growth. Surely the political ramifications of such questions are apparent.

"Inferences with Respect to Authoritative Behavior" are readily suggested by primate models on grounds of evolutionary theory. Particular attention has been given to this topic in such studies as Fred Willhoite's "Primates and Political Authority: A Biobehavioral Perspective" (1976) and Carol Barner-Barry's "The Biological Correlates of Power and Authority: Dominance and Attention Structure" (1978). The topic is discussed in the course by Fred Kort, and it can be seen that it follows appropriately the presentations by Harper on "Primate Evolution of Behavior," "Human Evolution," and "Being Human." It is noted in this context that Willhoite (1976) gives considerable attention to dominance-deference hierarchies in Old World monkeys and apes. He suggests that these hierarchies may have acquired special importance as a survival function in view of the rapid expansion of the brain in the evolution of primates. If so, relevance can be attributed to the study of politics in terms of models of authoritative behavior in primates.

Both Willhoite (1976) and Barner-Barry (1978) make clear that dominance-deference hierarchies are established not only by aggression, but perhaps more significantly by attention structure. Authoritative behavior and aggression have to be conceptually distinguished, therefore, and the discussion of "Aggression and International Relations" has to be accommodated separately. Before Norman Kogan addresses himself specifically to this topic in the course, Elizabeth Hanson gives a general presentation of "Biological Approaches to the Understanding of International Relations." She notes that the discipline of international relations is based on diversity and thus cannot ignore the diversity of humans. Ethology and the study of human evolution therefore are important for this discipline. Biological factors of war have received special attention, but—in considering these factors—it has to be noted that states go to war, and questions have to be raised regarding the extension of any possible biological explanation of individual behavior to the analysis of decision-making by collective entities.

Although Hanson refers to aggression, the primary attention to aggression in international relations is given in Kogan's presentation. He notes that the contemporary ethologists have avoided the errors of Social Darwinism, which—as has been seen—receive attention at the beginning of the course, but which certainly also require comment in the context of international relations. The necessary cautionary aspect in the research of the ethologists is that the empirical evidence of aggression is obtained from observations of nonhuman animals, and that, consequently, the important question arises: To what extent can inferences be made about humans? It is in this connection, of course, that the even more general questions regarding evolutionary development, such as those pertaining to homologies, have to be raised again. Quite independently, as Kogan points out, it has to be recognized that every civilization has a history of war. To what extent this phenomenon can be explained by biology and to what extent it is the result of particular cultural developments is indeed the subject of a persistent debate. In any case, it should be noted that biological development, and not only culture, has provided inhibitors of aggressive behavior.

It is quite understandable that of all behavioral components, a possible biological explanation of aggression has elicited interest in political science and—as just has been seen—particularly in the study of international relations. Of equal importance, however, is the concept of altruism, which has acquired a specific meaning in biology, but which—in this sense and not merely with its conventional meaning—has definite ramifications for political development. Accordingly, presentations on "Altruism as a Concept in Biological Literature" and "Altruism and Political Institutions and Procedures" are given in the course by Kort. It is made clear in this connection that the term "altruism" in biology basically refers to conduct pertaining to reproduction. It also is noted that a distinction must be made between the use of the term in relation to kin selection and its use in a much more encompassing sense, namely, as "reciprocal altruism"—a concept developed by Trivers (1971: 35-57). It is in the latter sense that the concept is of particular interest to the study of political institutions and procedures. The main types of human altruistic behavior that Trivers identifies—help in times of danger; sharing food; help to the sick, the wounded, the very young, and the very old; sharing implements; and sharing knowledge—have been institutionalized to varying degrees in politically organized societies, and procedures for their implementation have been created. On the basis of Trivers' model, then, political phenomena in even the technologically most advanced societies, ranging from national defense to social security and public education, may have to be understood in terms of evolution and genetics.

HUMAN DIVERSITY, SOMATIC STATES, AND THEIR IMPACT ON POLITICAL BEHAVIOR

In terms of a coordinate system, the evolutionary component of behavior can be visualized as a vertical dimension, and somatic states can be conceived as a horizontal dimension. An inversion of the dimensions would be equally justifiable as long as the conception of a coordinate system is maintained. Political behavior then can be represented by a third dimension and examined in relation to both the evolutionary perspective and somatic states.

A consideration of somatic states has to give proper recognition to human diversity, and human diversity in turn requires genetic explanation. For this reason, the first presentation in the part of the course devoted to somatic states and political behavior is given by Ginsburg on "Aspects of Behavior Genetics," corresponding to his presentation on "Genetic Aspects of Behavioral Evolution" in the context of the evolutionary perspective. It has been noted—in that context—that Ginsburg emphasizes the need for reexamining the assumptions of sociobiology as a foundation for a "new synthesis." For similar reasons, Ginsburg examines "The Concept of Biopolitics and Its Ramifications for a New Discipline." In both instances, considerations of behavior genetics precede these examinations.

A concern with somatic states and their influence on political behavior readily directs attention to the "Impact of Nutrition" and "Pharmacology and Its Ramifications." In the presentation of these topics in the course, Hana Dolezalova emphasizes not only the explanation of the relationship under consideration but also important policy questions that have been raised concerning nutrition and drugs. In this fashion the examination of somatic states, and behavior for obtaining explanation also suggests policy aspects, which receive special attention at the end of the course.

Before extending the discussion of somatic states and political behavior to psychophysiological variables in general terms, it is imperative to consider applicable studies of the central nervous system. Accordingly, Ginsburg devotes a presentation to "Studies of the Central Nervous System in Relation to Political Behavior." On this basis, two distinct relationships are examined. One is concerned with "Political Behavior as a Function of Psychophysiological Variables" and is discussed in a presentation by Kort. The other involves an inversion of the positions of dependent and independent variables in the preceding relationship and thus provides the topic for the discussion by Frederick Turner on "Psychophysiological Indicators as Functions of Political Variables." A noteworthy feature of this topic is the concern with the limitations of survey research, which has been used extensively in political science for several decades. Information derived from verbal responses in this technique may be enchanced considerably by the additional reliance on psychophysiological indicators.

POLICY FORMULATION IN ITS BIOLOGICAL CONTEXT AND UNDERLYING METHODOLOGICAL CONSIDERATIONS

Although conceptual frameworks for inquiry provide the initial topics of the course, specific methodological questions have to be examined before the policy ramifications of the interface between biology and politics can receive special attention. For this reason, Victor Denenberg devotes his first presentation to "Principles of Causality and General Systems Theory," and then proceeds in his second presentation to discuss "Social and Legal Implications of Different Theories of Determinism Derived from Biological and Behavioral Research." In this fashion, the emphasis on the caution of inference that characterizes the entire course is manifested again. Special caution is necessary at this point in the course, for the final topics of "Policy Formulation and Biological Considerations" and "Policy Implementations and Biological Boundaries"—which are discussed by Kort—are precarious. Diverse aspects of governmental responsibility with respect to policies and their relations to biological knowledge are noted in this discussion, with the recognition that these relations have special significance for the administration of criminal justice.

REFERENCES

ATZ, J. W. (1970) "The application of the idea of homology to behavior." In L. R. Aronson et al. (eds.) Development and Evolution of Behavior. San Francisco, CA: W. H. Freeman.

BARNER-BARRY, C. (1978) "The biological correlates of power and authority: dominance and attention structure." Presented at the annual meeting of the American Political Science Association.

BITTERMAN, M. E. (1965) "Phyletic differences in learning." Amer. Psychologist 20: 396-410.

CORNING, P. (1978) "Biopolitics: toward a new political science." Presented at the annual meeting of the American Political Science Association.

DARWIN, C. (1974) The Descent of Man. Reprint of the 1874 ed., Chicago: Rand McNally.

——— (1965) The Expression of Emotions in Man and Animals. Reprint ed. with preface by K. Lorenz. Chicago: Univ. of Chicago Press.

——— (1964) The Origin of Species. Reprint of 1859 ed., Cambridge, MA: Harvard Univ. Press.

HARLOW, H. F. (1949) "The formation of learning sets." Psych. Rev. 56: 51-65.

LOCHNER v. NEW YORK (1905) 198 U.S. 45.

LORENZ, K. (1971) Studies in Animal and Human Behavior, vols. 1 and 2. Cambridge, MA: Harvard Univ. Press.

SAGAN, C. (1977) The Dragons of Eden: Speculations on the Evolution of Human Intelligence. New York: Random House.

SOMIT, A. [ed.] (1976) Biology and Politics: Recent Explorations. Paris: Mouton.

SPENCER, H. (1893) Man Versus the State. New York: D. Appleton.

THORNDIKE, E. L. (1899) "The associative processes in animals." Biological Lectures of the Marine Biological Laboratory at Woods Hole 7: 69-81.

TINBERGEN, N. (1951) The Study of Instinct. New York: Oxford Univ. Press.

TRIVERS, R. L. (1971) "The evolution of reciprocal altruism." Q. Rev. of Biology 46: 35-57.

WILLHOITE, F. (1976) "Primates and Political Authority: A Biobehavioral Perspective." Amer. Pol. Sci. Rev. 70: 1110-1126.

Seymour Halleck
University of North Carolina

9

THE FUTURE OF
PSYCHIATRIC CRIMINOLOGY

From the time psychiatrists first involved themselves in the problems of criminology until the present, the value of their contributions has been debated. The controversy begins with psychiatry's approach to theoretical criminology. Biological and psychological theories of crime have tended to be global and naive. Although these theories have been more polemical than scientific, they have exerted enormous influence on those who demand "practical" solutions to the crime problem. Biological and psychological theories, based on the concept that criminals are a distinct "type," offer excellent rationalizations for oppressing minorities. The doctrine that the criminal is "mad," just like the doctrine that he is "bad," can be used to justify his incapacitation or extirpation (Hooten, 1939). To the extent our citizens believe that the cause of crime lies within the individual who broke the law, society can avoid confronting its own criminogenic tendencies (Halleck, 1971).

Substantial critiques can also be made of psychiatric involvement in the practical issues of criminology. Interventions designed to rehabilitate the criminal have had discouraging outcomes. There are certainly scattered instances of success with groups of offenders using pharmacological, behavioral, or psychotherapeutic intervention. But our results in the area of rehabilitation, while probably no worse than other approaches, are at best unimpressive (Martinson, 1974).

Psychiatrists have played an active role in assisting the criminal justice system in managing mentally ill defendents. We have long been, and still are, involved in determining many offenders' competency to stand trial, and a few offenders' possible lack of guilt by reason of insanity (Brooks, 1974; Slovenko, 1973). We also make predictions about the dangerousness of offenders which may influence the duration of their incarceration (Monahan, 1970). Whether such activities facilitate the administration of criminal justice or hinder it, or whether they help offenders or hurt them are, however, matters of continuous debate.

Psychiatrists also have been active in administrating programs for the criminally insane. Conceivably, medical administration of hospitals for the criminally insane adds a certain amount of humanity and rationality to this particular social control system. But the forensic hospital system still remains so backward and repressive that few psychiatrists would take pride in contributing to its maintenance. Nor can we take pride in our involvement in specialized treatment programs for classes of offenders labeled sex deviates or psychopaths. It is still unclear whether such programs are helpful or harmful, but few psychiatrists these days would cite them as triumphs, either of psychiatric effectiveness or psychiatric humanism.

Even our provision of ordinary mental health services to troubled offenders, which are not designed to further the specific goal of rehabilitation, has been unimpressive. Fewer and fewer mental health professionals are available to work with offenders who actually want help. The lack of adequate psychiatric and medical care remains one of the additional punishments imposed on those who have already lost their freedom.

In the defense of psychiatry, it must be acknowledged that nonpsychiatric criminologists have not been particularly helpful in facilitating psychiatric involvement in criminology. Naive psychiatric theories are attacked with a kind of relish that borders on overkill even when these theories are often not much worse than sociological or economic theories (Rennie, 1978). Even more troubling, whenever mental health professionals begin to demonstrate some efficiency in changing behaviors through sophisticated techniques of behavior control, many criminologists, who have always espoused a retributive approach to the criminal, condemn such techniques as immoral and unethical (Burt, 1974). It has always seemed paradoxical to me that those who will tolerate the gradual degradation of the criminal's personality through years of harsh punishment should suddenly emerge as moralists committed to the offender's psychological autonomy. Certainly, criminologists should be concerned about the ethics of behavior control, but the massive rejection of reasonably scientific experimentation with direct behavior modification, much like the rejection of psychiatric theory, borders on overkill.

While the courts have welcomed psychiatric testimony in the criminal justice process, it is highly questionable whether they either take this testimony seriously or rely on it in decision making. It is also questionable whether they should rely very heavily on psychiatric testimony. Insanity and competency are legal issues. The courts must consider many nonpsychiatric variables in resolving these issues and these variables are often more critical than psychiatric testimony (Halleck, 1967). Psychiatrists are welcome in the courtroom less as esteemed experts than as witnesses who loan a pseudo-scientific rationale for preserving the traditions of the legal system. Nor can psychiatrists be blamed for the state of our hospitals for the criminally insane. The primitive status of these institutions is a disgrace which must be shared by all of society. Finally, even our reluctance to provide services to offenders who volunteer for them is somewhat understandable since our correctional institutions have, as a rule, made it quite difficult for psychiatrists to work with offenders.

In spite of the failures of the past and the negativism of the present, psychiatry continues to exert some influence on criminology. Psychological and biological theories of crime fade away, but they have a persistent tendency to recur in new and modernized form. Whether we decry them as evidence of Neo-Lombrosianism or welcome them as new scientific discoveries, theories continue to emerge which suggest that some criminals have psychological and biological deficiencies. As the basic sciences underlying psychiatric practice become more methodologically sound, these theories are taken slightly more seriously. The involvement of the psychiatrist in the courtroom has certainly not diminished and whether we are useful or not, we are more welcome than ever as expert witnesses. Criminologists who have not kept up with the current status of psychiatry will also find that as a profession we have been somewhat humbled. We have taken a more careful look at the results of our work with noncriminal patients, and this new scientific perspective forces us to acknowledge that our results even with the mentally ill are modest indeed (Luborsky et al., 1975). We have also been put in a defensive posture with regard to our treatment of involuntary mental patients (Ennis and Emery, 1978). Psychiatrists have been so busy defending their customary practices that they have little time or energy to venture out to find new fields to conquer. Thus, we do not mourn the demise of indeterminate sentencing and specialized programs. Nor are we too shaken by reports that our rehabilitative programs have not been very successful. Psychiatrists have enough to do keeping their own house in order and are more willing to accept the reality that their contributions to a field such as criminology will be limited.

The current relationship of psychiatry to criminology is most easily described as involving three major functions. First, the psychiatrist helps determine the disposition of offenders through cooperation with the courts or correctional institutions. Second, the psychiatrist develops explanations of human behavior which are transmitted to those who deal directly with the crime problem. Third, the psychiatrist treats offenders who are in effect defined as patients.

Our dispositional functions primarily involve assisting the courts in determining the individual offender's competency to stand trial or guilt or lack of guilt by reason of insanity. This function is rapidly expanding. Forensic psychiatry, unlike psychiatric criminology, is a growing field. The American Academy of Psychiatry and Law, founded only ten years ago, now has over 600 members. There are now several journals devoted to forensic psychiatry and the field has defined itself as a subspecialty with certification requirements. Of course, forensic psychiatry encompasses more than work with the criminal justice system, but competency and insanity hearings continue to make up a substantial part of the forensic psychiatrist's work.

The social usefulness of psychiatric involvement in legal decisions involving the criminal has been thoroughly questioned. Some fear that offenders' rights are compromised when they are found incompetent or insane (Szasz, 1963). Others (Dershowitz, 1973) believe that these adjudications enable offenders to "beat the rap." The theoretical basis for psychiatric involvement in insanity and competency to stand trial rulings is also questionable. To be competent to stand trial, an accused offender must be able to understand the charges against him, know the consequences of guilt, and be able to assist his attorney in his own defense. In recent years, as a number of convictions have been overturned because of failure to enter an incompetency plea, the use of that plea has become more frequent and almost routine in instances in which there are bizarre circumstances involved in a crime (Halpern, 1977). The plea may be entered by the defense, by the court, or by the prosecution, and is in fact more frequently raised by the court or the prosecution than by the defense (Slovenko, 1977).

As defined above, the criteria for competency are legal, not psychiatric. Whatever role psychiatrists can logically play in determining an individual's ability to understand charges or cooperate with his attorney is unclear. Yet, the courts continue to view this form of competency determination as a psychiatric function and too often psychiatrists eagerly accept this responsibility. Psychiatrists continue to define individuals as incompetent to stand trial primarily on the basis of mental illness and many courts continue to accept these recommendations without question (Halpern, 1977). There is great waste in this process. Offenders are sometimes hurt and public needs are not always met. Psychiatrists make statements which go far beyond their expertise. And the courts continue to perpetuate the myth of psychiatric expertise to rationalize the maintenance of a judicial status quo. Very gradually, but inexorably, attorneys, criminologists and some psychiatrists are beginning to call for substantial modifications or abolishment of the incompetency processing (Burt and Morris, 1972).

Until recently, the existence of the insanity defense had few practical consequences. Insanity pleas were rarely raised because offenders found not guilty by reason of insanity would usually be confined to hospitals for the criminally insane for about the same amount of time as if they had been found guilty. But with a new civil liberties movement which has successfully persuaded the courts to rule that people not guilty by reason of insanity should be treated like anyone else who is mentally ill, it has become clear that the insanity defense can become an efficient means of avoiding punishment (Singer, A. C., 1978). Thus, in many states, these pleas are increasing in frequency and the judiciary as well as the public is alarmed about the potential abuse of the insanity defense.

Whether our society needs an insanity defense or not is now being reconsidered cautiously (Stone, 1976). At the same time, psychiatrists should also ask themselves if they have anything to contribute to the judicial determination of insanity. My own opinion is that whatever standards are used in determining insanity, the psychiatrist is regularly asked to answer questions which relate more to value and opinion than to science. Responding to the M'Naughton or ALI standards requires that the psychiatrist make a statement about the offender's responsibility or accountability for his criminal action. There is absolutely no science that assists the psychiatrist in making such a statement.

This may be a useful time to digress and consider questions which have plagued criminology, and particularly psychiatric criminology, for centuries. "Are there people who should not be considered responsible for criminal behavior? Should the existence of mental illness be mitigative in imposing responsibility?" Let me propose a way of thinking about this problem that might demonstrate the absurdity of trying to determine scientifically who is responsible for a given act and who is not. I assume a deterministic model of human behavior. All behavior is determined by an individual's interaction with the environment; namely, by who an individual is both genetically and by virtue of previous learning experiences, and by how that individual is affected by the environment in which he exists at a given moment. There are many factors related to the individual's past learning and present environment that will influence his behavior. One of the most important is the demand, made by others, to behave responsibly. People are given messages in early childhood that they will be rewarded if they behave in certain ways and punished if they do not. They also learn to reward themselves if they behave in ways which they learn to deem compatible with "goodness" and to punish themselves if they behave "badly" (Thoreson and Mahoney, 1974). Society constantly offers similar rewards and punishments in the present. In almost all societies, the individual is taught to believe that he can exercise choice in determining how he will behave. This belief influences behavior in a deterministic manner just like any other educative device.

Responsibility is best considered an artificial construct or myth we impose on people to influence or determine their behavior in a direction we conceive desirable. The expectation that people behave responsibly is simply another factor which determines behavior. At the same time, I do not wish to imply that society can live without this myth. Society must demand that people behave responsibly so that it can shape (or determine) behavior. It must devise moral codes for determining who should be punished and who should not. Society can do all of these things, but it can never develop a scientific system for determining who is responsible and who is not.

This is not to say that there are no conditions which limit an individual's capacity to behave in an adaptive, law-abiding way. In many instances, poverty, oppression, and mental illness might limit an individual's choices. We may not want to punish offenders whose choices are limited as harshly as we punish those who may have broader opportunities. But, this has nothing to do with whether or not they are responsible for their actions. As a hypothetical construct, responsibility is not a quality that an individual either has or does not have. Psychiatrists cannot possibly state that a given individual is responsible or not responsible for a given crime. When psychiatrists testify at insanity trials, they are expressing moral, not scientific, opinions.

Another dispositional role for psychiatrists is their prediction of future dangerousness of offenders. In past years, parole boards often asked psychiatrists to examine certain inmates and comment on their potential dangerousness. Offenders serving indeterminate sentences were evaluated to make similar predictions. With the decline of indeterminate sentencing and specialized treatment programs, these activities will undoubtedly diminish. Although much has been written about this subject, it remains unclear whether such activities were of much value in protecting society, and it is equally unclear how harmful they actually were to the rights of offenders. Psychiatrists (as well as many other people) can, with common sense, actuarial data, and clinical skills, determine that certain offenders are at greater risk of commiting violent offenses than others. It is clear that some people are more dangerous than others and we have some skills in defining who these people are. But what we cannot do, with very much accuracy, is predict a dangerous act in a given individual (Monahan, 1973). If everyone who had a greater likelihood than the average person to commit a violent offense were subject to a restrictive sanction, the number of people falsely and unnecessarily penalized would be overwhelming (Ennis and Emery, 1978). All of this should direct psychiatrists to continue to study the issue of predicting violence, but to caution them and others not to take their predictions too seriously. There is little likelihood that our limited contributions in this area will expand in the near future.

Moving away from our dispositional functions, the future of psychiatry's theoretical or educational contributions seems brighter. The history of criminology suggests that efforts to find biological and psychological explanations of crime will never stop. I see no reason why they should. Some psychological insights explain a small amount of criminal behavior. Psychiatrists' general knowledge of human behavior should exceed that of the lay person's. We are often able to present insights to the police officer, to the judge, or to the prison official which assist them in dealing with the offender. As long as psychiatrists are not too grandiose or arrogant in providing explanations of human behavior, their ideas are usually welcomed with considerable enthusiasm by workers in corrections. They may even be useful.

If we take a systems approach to explanation, it is relatively easy to integrate certain psychobiological ideas into theoretical criminology. Of course, psychiatric insights, like those of any other field, are limited largely to a small proportion of criminals; namely, those who happen to get caught, convicted, and subjected to some form of social control. In defending the usefulness of psychiatric theory, I want to emphasize that I agree with most criminologists that there can be no single explanation for crime and that politics and economics are major issues in causing crime. I have no argument with Norval Morris' statement that "The causes of human behavior are the causes of crime" (Morris and Hawkins, 1970). It seems clear that a free society will have more crime than a totalitarian society. It also seems clear that a free society which is affluent, but characterized by alienation, lack of purpose, and lack of compassion, will have more crime than one that is not. In short, a society experiences the kind of crime it deserves and I have no illusions that psychobiological models will have a substantial effect in dealing with the problem of crime.

As a psychiatrist, however, I am distressed at the naive and cavalier way in which psychobiological insights may be dismissed because they are associated with the "medical model." There should, in my opinion, be a special place in purgatory for those who use the term "medical model" without defining it. For many reasons that are more propagandistic than scientific, writers in criminology seem to feel obligated to begin their dissertations with a polemical attack against the medical model. (Just as psychiatrists begin theirs with a plea for returning to it.) You will forgive me if I digress for a moment and try and point out that the concept of "medical model" is actually quite complicated.

One way in which the medical model can be conceptualized is to view it as a method of explaining organismic activity that is maladaptive either to the individual or to those around him. Explanations of this behavior can be reductionistic or systems-oriented (Whybrow, 1972). It is true that in medicine we often search for a single biological defect to explain a particular aberration of human activity. There is a certain efficiency and crispness to this reductionist approach. But even the most "hard line" biologists know that single factor explanations are insufficient for understanding disease or deviation. There is a strong, new trend in medicine to view organismic dysfunction as the result of many interacting variables, including current environmental influences (Engel, 1960). It is not too farfetched to argue that by using explanations derived from a systems model of mental illness, Norval Morris' phrase could be changed to read "The causes of human behavior are the causes of illness." Thus, when criminologists reject the systems model, they are in effect rejecting important aspects of their own models.

The medical model can also be viewed as a way of defining relationships between two parties who have some need to do business with one another. The medical model assumes:

(a) that one person needs help and the other can help.
(b) that the helper must have some power over the person helped.
(c) that with this power comes some responsibility to help the other person in accordance with certain ethical precepts, namely, the doctor (or helper) has a fiduciary or trustee relationship in which he must always look out for the welfare of the other person.
(d) that the helping relationship must be characterized by an ethic of "above all, do no harm."
(e) that the helping relationship must be based on hope.
(f) that the relationship should end when the help is provided.

I suspect that when criminologists reject the medical model, they are largely concerned about the paternalistic way in which the relationship between the helper and the helped is defined. But most other aspects of the above defined relationship would probably not be rejected by most criminologists. Nor should they be rejected.

We have heard Professor Jeffery apply psychobiological insights to the problem of punishment (Jeffery, 1978). Psychobiology can also be applied to the idea of risk-benefit evaluation, or the idea that the criminal will rationally assess the potential benefits and risk of a given act before committing it. Using a broad based phenomenological and psychoanalytic (as well as behavioral) perspective, the risk-benefit paradigm can be expanded in three ways. First, risk-benefit evaluation may not take place entirely on a conscious level, and some of the decision making process may be outside of the individual's awareness. Second, when we talk about risk-benefit evaluation, we should also consider that the individual evaluates the psychological risks and benefits he takes as defined by his particular internalized reward and punishment systems (Kadzin, 1975). We do not evaluate the consequences of an act simply by the way it will influence the responses of others. We also evaluate the consequences in terms of how it will influence our treatment of ourselves. Third, we must acknowledge that disturbances of perception will at times lead to individuals distorting risk-benefit ratios.

There are a number of psychobiological explanations of why an individual may come to unduly value the benefits of a criminal act. First, the individual may have biological limitations which interfere with his capacity to gratify needs through legitimate means. Individuals who are mentally defective or who have learning disorders may be unsuccessful in gratifying normal needs for status, power, and money. They may exaggerate the benefits of criminal activities because nothing else is open to them. (This concept is similar to sociological theories of crime which were popular in the 1960s [Cloward and Ohlin, 1963].) Second, the early learning experiences may be so distorted that one learns to unduly value certain activities. People exposed early in life to an environment in which violence is regularly used to resolve conflict will overvalue the benefits of violence. People whose early learning is distorted in some way, so that their sexual gratifications are directed toward inappropriate goals or objects, overvalue the benefits of deviant sexual activity. It is also possible that some biological disorders, by increasing aggressive and sexual drives, may leave the individual in a situation where he has an exaggerated view of the benefits of certain forms of violent behavior. Conceivably, individuals with types of epileptic disorders which are classified under the syndrome of episodic dyscontrol may experience this kind of distortion of the benefits of violence (Mark and Ervin, 1970).

There are other possible situations in which the capacity to weigh benefits against risks is seriously impaired. Certainly, people whose brain functioning is impaired cannot assess adequately the risks and benefits of the criminal act. This is especially true when brain functioning is impaired by abuse of alcohol. The percentage of crimes committed when people are drunk is amazingly high no matter what set of statistics are used (Hollis, 1974). But criminals (at least those that get caught and whom we can study) are not only likely to be intoxicated at the time of the crime, but also have a high incidence of chronic alcoholism. The addiction itself may play a role in eroding their capacity to evaluate risks and benefits. Individuals who are experiencing a major psychosis will, of course, have an impairment of their capacity to assess benefits and risks. This is especially true of the bipolar affective illnesses usually referred to as manic depressive psychosis. And it is certainly conceivable that some of the subtle biological changes which have been at times noted in those people we call psychopaths, and who are alleged to have a high propensity toward criminality, may play some role in impairing their capacity to evaluate both the benefits and the risks of criminality (Hare, 1970).

It would seem that an enlightened criminology would continue to want more data on psychological and biological variables which influence risk-benefit assessment. As long as psychiatrists seek reasonable goals, and are modest about the extent to which their contributions will influence criminology, there is room for many lifetimes of research in defining the influence of psychobiological variables in criminal behavior.

In turning to the third area of psychiatric involvement, treatment and rehabilitation, it is again important that criminologists be precise in defining these terms. Treatment can be defined either as certain activities one person engages in while trying to influence another, or the specific goals of the activity. Using the latter approach, there might be four conceivable goals in "treating" an offender.

I. Do something to the offender that will diminish the probabilities of his committing crimes, and do not be concerned whether the actions taken to change him are painful to him or compromise his future potentialities to function comfortably and effectively in society.

II. Do something to diminish an individual's probability of committing further crimes, but do this without harming the individual in any way or diminishing his future potentialities.

III. Do something to diminish the probabilities that an individual will commit future crimes, but at the same time try to ascertain that the interventions will leave the person even more capable of functioning comfortably and effectively in society than he functioned before he was treated.

IV. Do something to the individual to make the offender more comforable and effective, and do not be concerned what effect the intervention has upon the offender's subsequent criminal behavior.

It will be apparent that goals I, II, and III are all definitions of rehabilitation as well as of treatment. They certainly have profoundly different ethical meanings and consequences for the offender, but when we talk loosely about treatment and rehabilitation, we could be talking about any of these goals. It should also be apparent that if we are concerned only with goal I, diminishing criminal potentiality without any regard for the needs of the offender, there is a great deal that we can do right now to rehabilitate offenders. To put this argument in its most barbaric form, we could rehabilitate most offenders by cutting off their hands, castrating them, or resorting to some other form of physical mutilation. Psychiatrists could make an immediate contribution to diminishing the opportunities of offenders to commit subsequent crimes by incapacitating them through use of psychosurgery and long-acting psychotropic drugs such as prolixin. We reject these "rehabilitative" efforts on ethical grounds.

More excruciating questions will face us when we develop drugs which may diminish the propensity or possibility of criminality while imposing less drastic harm on the individual. Perhaps, some of these goals can already be accomplished through existing forms of behavior modification, but even combinations of drugs and behavior modification as used today probably do some damage to the individual. Ultimately, however, our technologies will get better. They will then provide a more efficient means of control under goal II, which is to prevent crime without harm to the offender. While our society and professional criminologists as well as attorneys have rarely been terribly concerned about how offenders are brutalized through incarceration, they seem, as previously noted, to draw the line at behavior control through medical technology. Whether they will maintain this stance forever is debatable. As technologies become less barbaric and as the cost of keeping people in jail for long periods of time becomes too burdensome, there may be some modification of these attitudes.

Currently, most mental health professionals who work in the correctional area would like to believe that goal III, diminishing the probability of criminal behavior while leaving the individual better off is the most desirable; we have also found it to be the most elusive goal. Psychiatrists are now taking a more careful look at the possibility that the proper role of the psychiatrist may be primarily that of goal IV. Perhaps, the psychiatrist should simply try to help the offender without worrying about whether such efforts rehabilitate the offender. There are certainly many offenders who need and would volunteer for psychiatric attention independently of the question of their reformation. The experience of imprisonment in itself leads to a high incidence of depression. Many prisoners, just like people outside of prison, are mentally ill and need treatment. Once the psychiatrist could be defined as somebody who is trying to help offenders without concern for their rehabilitation, there would be less justification for making the psychiatrist a member of the correctional system and in jeopardy of functioning as a double agent (Szasz, 1963). Private psychiatrists might then be able to contract to treat prisoners just as they treat other patients. The psychiatrist would not be responsible to the prison institution. All of this might be accomplished by a form of national health insurance which provided the same benefits to incarcerated criminals as to anyone else.

This raises the interesting question of whether prisoners have a right to treatment. My impression is that if indeterminate sentencing models are allowed to continue, the case for a right to treatment will remain strong. Some offenders are denied freedom because they cannot receive disorders. If there is treatment for these disorders and if offenders are denied freedome because they cannot receive it, a good case can be made that their constitutional rights under the eighth and fourteenth Amendments are being violated. With the advent of determinate sentencing, the case for a right to treatment will certainly be much more difficult to make.

Before leaving the topic of treatment, something should be said about the related area of prevention. Society can probably do at least a little to prevent crime without drastically changing its social structures. Psychiatrists can help at least a little in this process. Certainly, the treatment of learning disorders in children, the protection of children from violence, and the creation of relatively wholesome environments in which virtually abandoned children can be given a certain degree of nurturance should help prevent a small amount of crime.

For psychiatrists and anyone else interested in the crime problem, our current era is dominated by long overdue realism. We know that thus far our efforts at rehabilitation have not been very effective and nobody has any illusions that rehabilitation of apprehended offenders, even if made much more effective, would significantly influence the crime problem. There is also little evidence that severe retribution will have a significant influence in reducing crime (Doleschal, 1977). If there is any deterrent effect to punishment (and this is still questionable), it is more likely to be related to certainty and celerity of punishment, not to severity (Bailey et al., 1974). It is becoming increasingly clear that even massive incapacitation of allegedly dangerous offenders would have only a minimal impact on reducing the rate of violent crime (Dinitz and Conrad, 1978). And we know that even if we could apprehend more criminals (which is unlikely), our court system could not possibly process them; and if for some reason they could, our prisons could not possibly hold them without bankrupting state budgets.

One aspect of our new realism is an effort to stop trying to do anything spectacular and to concentrate simply on providing justice. A major and highly popular consequence of this attitude has been a demand that we shift to determinate or presumptive sentencing (Singer, R., 1978). As one who has always favored determinate maximum sentences and indeterminate minimum sentences, I find little refreshing, exciting, or useful about the new approach. It may ultimately prove to be more fair to these offenders who happen to go to prison (who, in comparison with other offenders, have always been treated unfairly), but I strongly doubt if it will make prisons quieter places or make prisoners more contented clients. The determinate sentencing laws which are currently being enacted leave powerful discretionary loopholes through plea bargaining and provide prison officials with the power to regulate good time (Clear et al., 1978). Even more discouraging, determinate sentencing seems to be associated with a philosophy of "making the sentences" stiff. The alliance of academicians and politicians in pushing for determinate sentencing is not an alliance of equals. The ultimate power belongs to the politicians who are profoundly influenced by what they perceive to be the retributionist attitude of the public and who will exploit whatever theory fits their needs. The temporary glory an academician may grasp by enunciating a doctrine that happens to meet the political needs of the moment is probably obtained at the expense of wasted human and societal resources.

The reality of the limited capability of our society to do very much to control crime is depressing. But it can also be liberating. If there is little we can do, we can certainly stop wasting our time with extravagant claims that various actions can solve the crime problem. We can cease to provide legislators with rationalizations for taking popular but dangerously ineffective actions. In addition to continuing to study crime, our only obligations should be in the direction of developing a value system in which we, first, seek to do no further harm and second, treat both the victims and perpetrators of criminal actions as decently as possible. Such a moral stance would call for actions which I am sure many of you would endorse with little hesitation.

(1) We should pay much less attention to victimless crime and drastically reduce the punishment for such crime.

(2) We should strive to make prisons decent, safe places, characterized by a certain amount of justice, industry, and hope.

(3) We should focus on victim-oriented punishment and seek to expand the use of models of restitution.

(4) We should stop providing rationales for sentencing offenders to cruel and absurdly prolonged sentences.

In addition to our other research activities, we should begin to investigate why society's response to criminality remains so consistently irrational. In spite of overwhelming evidence to the contrary, it is probably true that the majority of the American people and most of their leaders believe that the crime problem can be solved by either "getting tougher" or by expanding rehabilitation. The psychological devices by which such illusions are maintained are not adaptive. Whatever kind of social system maintains the mythology which dominates the American attitude towards crime needs definition and explanation. Those who continue to hold false beliefs in spite of continued and convincing evidence that they are wrong, are in desparate need of, if you will pardon the expression, treatment and rehabilitation.

REFERENCES

BAILEY, W. C., S. D. MARTIN, and L. N. GRAY (1974) "Crime and deterrence: a correctional analysis." J. of Research in Crime and Delinquency (July): 124-143.

BROOKS, A. D. (1974) Law, Psychiatry and the Mental Health System. Boston: Little Brown.

BURT, R. (1974) "Of mad dogs and scientists: the perils of the criminally insane." University of Pennsylvania Law Rev. 123, 258.

CLEAR, T. R., J. D. HEWITT, and R. M. REGOLI (1978) Discretion and the determinate sentence: its distribution, control, and effect on time served." Crime and Delinquency 24 (October): 428-445.

CLOWARD, R. and L. E. OHLIN (1963) Delinquency and Opportunity. Glencoe: Free Press.

DERSHOWITZ, A. (1973) "Abolishing the insanity defense: the most significant feature of the administration's proposed code." Criminal Law Bulletin 9.

DINITZ, S. and J. CONRAD (1978) "Thinking about dangerous offenders." Criminal Justice Abstracts (March). 99-130.

DOLESCHAL, E. (1977) "Rates and length of imprisonment." Crime and Delinquency 23, 51-56.

ENGEL, G. (1960) "A unified concept of health and disease." Perspectives in Biological Medicine 3, 459.

ENNIS, B. J. and R. D. EMERY (1978) The Rights of Mental Patients. New York: Avon.

HALLECK, S. L. (1971) The Politics of Therapy. New York: Science House, 1971.

——— (1967) Psychiatry and the Dilemma of Crime. New York: Harper & Row.

HALPERN, A. (1977) "Uses and misuses of psychiatry in competency examination of criminal defendants." In Diagnosis and Debate. New York: Insight Communications.

HARE, R. D. (1970) Psychopathy: Theory and Research. New York: John Wiley.

HOLLIS, W. S. (1974) "On the etiology of criminal homicides—the alcohol factor." J. of Police Sci. and Administration 2, 50-51.

HOOTON, E. A. (1939) The American Criminal: An Anthropological Study. Cambridge, MA: Harvard Univ. Press.

JEFFERY, C. R. (1979) "Punishment and deterrence: a psychobiological statement." Presented at the meeting of the American Society of Criminology, Dallas, Texas, November 8-12.

KAZDIN, A. E. (1975) Behavior Modification in Applied Settings. Homewood: Dorsey Press.

LUBORSKY, R., B. SINGER, and L. LUBORSKY (1975) "Comparative studies of psychotherapy." Archives of General Psychiatry 32, 995-1208.

MARK, V. H. and F. ERVIN (1970) Violence and the Brain. New York: Harper & Row.

MARTINSON, R. (1974) "What works? questions and answers about prison reform." Public Interest (Spring).

MONAHAN, J. (1973) "Dangerous offender: a critique of Kozel et al." Crime and Delinquency 19, 418-419.

MORRIS, N. and G. HAWKINS (1970) The Honest Politicians Guide to Crime Control. Chicago: Univ. of Chicago Press.

RENNIE, Y. (1978) The Search for Criminal Man. Lexington: D. C. Heath.

SINGER, A. C. (1978) "Insanity acquittal in the seventies: observations and empirical analysis of one jurisdiction." Mental Disability Law 4, 406-417.

SINGER, R. (1978) "In favor of presumptive sentences set by a sentencing commission." Crime and Delinquency 24 (October): 401-427.

SLOVENKO, R. (1977) "The developing law on competency to stand trial." J. of Psychiatry and Law (Summer): 165-201.

——— (1973) Psychiatry and Law. Boston: Little, Brown.

STONE, A. (1976) "Mental health and the law: a system in transition." Report of the National Institutes of Mental Health.

SZASZ, T. (1963) Law, Liberty and Psychiatry. New York: Macmillan.

THORESON, T. E. and M. J. MAHONEY (1974) Behavioral Self Control. New York: Holt, Rinehart and Winston.

WHYBROW, P. C. (1972) "The use and abuse of the medical model as a conceptual framework in psychiatry." Psychiatry in Medicine 3, 33-361.

ABOUT THE AUTHORS

HARRY E. ALLEN is professor, Department of Administration of Justice, San Jose State University, San Jose, California. Previously, he was Professor and Director, Program for the Study of Crime and Delinquency, Ohio State University. His current research interests include parole, community-based corrections, probation, and evaluation research.

ERIC W. CARLSON is an Assistant Professor of Public Administration at the University of Arizona, Tucson. The reported research was conducted while he was the Associate Director of the Ohio State University Program for the Study of Crime and Delinquency. His current interests include research in probation, parole, community corrections centers, and policy analysis methodologies.

PATRICK S. DYNES is a doctoral candidate and Graduate Research Associate in the Program for the Study of Crime and Delinquency, School of Public Administration, the Ohio State University. His research interests include criminal careers, corrections, and probation.

BENSON E. GINSBURG, currently Professor and Head of the Department of Biobehavioral Sciences at the University of Connecticut, Storrs, received his Ph.D. from the University of Chicago in 1943. He was twice a fellow at the Center for Advanced Study in the Behavioral Sciences at Stanford; was William Rainy Harper Professor of Biology at the University of Chicago; and came to the University of Connecticut to form a new multidisciplinary department, which he heads, and within which he chairs the Behavioral Genetics Laboratory. His major interest is the genetic regulation of neural and endocrine events in development as they interface with environmental factors. These are being studied at the genic and chromosomal level in mice, at the behavioral and physiological levels in wild and domestic Canids, and at the level of building genetic taxonomies for human behavioral syndromes using marker techniques. His research publications have appeared in: *Behavior Genetics, Psychopharmacology, Neurochemical Research, Hormones and Behavior, Endocrinology, Life Sciences, Brain Research, Biochemical Pharmacology,* and *Epilepsia.*

SEYMOUR HALLECK received his medical training at the University of Chicago and his psychiatric training at the Menninger School of Psychiatry. He has served as a psychiatrist in a number of clinical and correctional settings, and currently he is Professor of Psychiatry at the University of North Carolina Medical School.

Dr. Halleck has been a forensic psychiatrist and has published a number of articles and books in this area, including *Psychiatry and the Dilemma of Crime, The Politics of Therapy, The Addine Annual of Crime and Criminal Justice, 1973-1974* (editor), and *The Treatment of Emotional Disorders.* He was the 1978 recipient of the Sutherland Award from the American Society of Criminology. His article "The Future of Psychiatric Criminology" was his Sutherland address to the Society.

HAROLD R. HOLZMAN recently completed his doctoral studies in Criminal Justice and Criminology at the University of Maryland. He is presently working in the Office of Program Evaluation, National Institute of Law Enforcement and Criminal Justice, LEAA. The paper published in this volume is Dr. Holzman's initial foray into Biological Criminology and was prompted by constant exposure to his wife's trials and tribulations as a teacher of special education in the primary grades. The phenomenology of deviance, which he believes includes biological as well as social and psychological dimensions, is one of his major research interests.

C. R. JEFFERY, Professor of Criminology at Florida State University and 1978 president of the American Society of Criminology, was recipient of the Edwin Sutherland Award of the Society, and has received a Fulbright-Hays award for the Netherlands for 1978-1979. He is author of numerous works, including *Crime Prevention Through Environmental Design,* and is a former editor of *Criminology: An Interdisciplinary Journal.*

HENRY E. KELLY, presently on sabbatical, is a member of the sociology faculty at the University of Tulsa.

FRED KORT is professor of political science at the University of Connecticut. He received his Ph.D. from Northwestern University in 1950. He has written articles for journals in political science and law reviews, and he has contributed major chapters to the volumes on *Judicial Decision-Making* and *Mathematical Applications in Political Science.* In connection with his specialties in the study of judicial behavior and the application of quantitative methods in political science, he developed his interest in the biological foundations of political behavior.

STEPHEN C. MAXSON is an Associate Professor in the Departments of Biobehavioral Sciences and Psychology at the University of Connecticut, Storrs. He received his Ph.D. in 1966 from the University of Chicago. His major research interests include the inheritance of behavior in mice and genetic mapping of behavioral loci; genotype-environment interactions in neurobehavioral development; pharmacogenetics of behavior; genetics, development, physiology, and pharmacology of aggressive behavior and audiogenic and spontaneous seizures; and behavior as an assay for potentially mutagenic and teratogenic substances. His research publications have appeared in *Nature; Behavioral Genetics; Psychopharmacologia (Berlin); Pharmacology, Biochemistry and Behavior; Experimental Neurology;* and *Life Sciences.*

KENNETH MOYER received his bachelor's degree from Park College and his Ph.D. from Washington University. After completion of the Ph.D., Dr. Moyer joined the faculty of the Carnegie Institute of Technology. He is currently Professor of Psychology at Carnegie-Mellon University. In 1954 Professor Moyer served as a consultant on higher education to the government of Norway. He is a fellow of the Division of Psychopharmacology, American Psychological Association, and a fellow of the American Association for the Advancement of Science. In addition to numerous scientific articles, Dr. Moyer has written: *The Physiology of Hostility, You and Your Child—A Primer for Parents, The Physiology of Aggression and Implications for Control, The Psychobiology of Aggression* (with J. M. Crabtree), *Bibliography of Aggressive Behavior: A Readers Guide to the Research Literature,* and *Neuroanatomy: Text and Illustrations.*